A Humanizing Dual Language Immersion Education

A Humanizing Dual Language Immersion Education

By

Yvette V. Lapayese

BRILL

SENSE

LEIDEN | BOSTON

All chapters in this book have undergone peer review.

The Library of Congress Cataloging-in-Publication Data is available online at http://catalog.loc.gov

Typeface for the Latin, Greek, and Cyrillic scripts: "Brill". See and download: brill.com/brill-typeface.

ISBN 978-90-04-38970-0 (paperback)
ISBN 978-90-04-38971-7 (hardback)
ISBN 978-90-04-38972-4 (e-book)

To my three sons,
Diego, Carlo, and Marco,
who each embrace Spanish and English differently,
with unique intensity and care.

∵

Contents

Introduction

In every corner of the world, young children are learning languages at home that differ from the dominant language used in their broader social world. These children arrive at school with a precious resource: their mother tongue.

In the face of this resource and the possibility for biliteracy, minority and indigenous language children learn the language of the majority group in their schools to fit in socially and succeed academically (Arnold, Bartlett, Gowani, & Merali, 2006; Wolff & Ekkehard, 2000). These majority language educational programs do nothing to support minority language children in developing competence in their primary language. Moreover, the language policies that inform these programs devalue the cultural backgrounds and knowledge associated with minority children's mother tongue.

Instead of adding to it, monolingual education subtracts from the children's linguistic repertoire. Linguistic minority children undergoing this type of education are forcibly transferred to the dominant group both linguistically and culturally. The most decisive educational factor causing negative statistics of linguistic minority 'performance' is the use of the wrong teaching language, together with a lack of meaningful content, methods, and ethos in schools. This subtractive education causes mental and physical harm; both are defined as genocide in the United Nations Genocide Convention.

Research confirms that children learn best in their mother tongue as a prelude to and complement of bilingual and multilingual education. The growing interest in mother tongues coincides with political movements seeking greater inclusiveness, rights, and dignity of minority communities. To counter monolingual education, there are significant albeit very few initiatives around the world that provide formal support for children to continue to develop competence in their mother tongue, while also learning an additional language or languages (UNESCO, 2000). One such initiative is dual language immersion education (DLI).

The U.S. Department of Education (2015) defines two main models of dual language programs:

- Two-way dual language programs, in which ELs who are fluent in the partner language and English-speaking peers are integrated to receive instruction in both English and the partner language.
- One-way dual language programs, in which students from predominantly one language group receive instruction in both English and a partner language. One-way dual language programs may serve predominantly ELs (also known as developmental or maintenance bilingual programs); predominantly English-speaking students (also known as one-way/world

language immersion programs); or predominantly students with a family background or cultural connection to the partner language (also known as heritage or native language programs).

For the purpose of the book, I focus specifically on the first model, two-way dual language immersion (DLI) programs. DLI education sets out to sustain and develop the language resources that children bring with them. For one, DLI programs do not view students' heritage or home language as a deficit. Students receive instruction in their primary language, thus beginning their academic journey in a language they are already familiar with. Secondly, DLI de-segregates language minority children from their English-speaking counterparts. Research suggests that the presence of these two groups together can lead to more inter-group communicative competence and a stronger sense of cultural awareness for both groups.

In the United States, despite the fact that research overwhelmingly supports DLI education, issues surrounding race, immigration, and power fuel an English-only ideology that continues to undercut policies and practices that support bilingual education. That said, a grassroots movement to build DLI programs and schools in states like California, where a significant number of language learners reside, is gaining momentum. This has resulted in the recent passage of Proposition 58 (Multilingual Initiative) in 2017, which reinstated bilingual education in California.

These are exciting times for our linguistic minoritized[1] youth as research and organizations dedicated to supporting DLI education feel the increasing popularity and growth of DLI programs across the country. Although the goals of DLI vary at each school, most tend to share some basic similarities. The mission of all DLI schools is to develop bilingual, biliterate, and multicultural students. Language minoritized students are expected to become literate in their primary language as well as in the dominant language. English-dominant language students should make the same progress in their native language development and content areas as they would in any school while simultaneously becoming proficient and literate in a second language. Lastly, bilingual youth develop intercultural competencies and multicultural understandings through the learning of languages.

Significance

Interestingly, most (if not all) research on DLI programs focus on the *effectiveness* of bilingual education vis-à-vis academic access and achievement. Scholars tends to argue and reargue, cite and recite, the pedagogical advantageousness of bilingual methodologies and methods for linguistic minoritized youth to succeed in U.S. schools, ultimately debunking the merits of English-only education. This book contends that the present ideology(ies) embedded in the research and guidelines for DLI education, albeit necessary and critical during the early days of DLI schooling, are disconnected from the present realities, epistemologies, and humanness of our bilingual youth. We are witnessing both stimulating and challenging times to push forth a new DLI framework, one that is holistic and that at its core, challenges the underpinnings of traditional schooling corrupted by assessment and accountability measures which dehumanize children—in this case, bilingual children.

The book envisions a new DLI framework informed by bilingual teachers and students who support biliteracy as a human right. Positioning bilingual education under a human rights framework allows us to address the basic right of our bi/multilingual youth to human dignity. Language is not only a tool for communication and knowledge, but also a fundamental attribute of cultural identity and empowerment—both for the individual and the group. Cultural groups realize the need to ensure the transmission of their linguistic heritage to the youngest members of their communities (UNESCO, 2008). Respect for the languages of persons belonging to different linguistic communities is therefore essential to a just and democratic society. Given the centrality of language to self-identification, our sense of who we are, and where we fit in the broader world, a connection between linguistic human rights and bilingual education is essential.

Nuancing Human Rights

Scholars have exposed 'human rights' false claims to universality, its investment in and reproduction of a narrow liberal ontology, its inability to break with global capitalist ordering, its indebtedness to and repetition of colonial history, and a host of other related criticisms. In short, the critique of human rights as a particular form of Western political liberalism that gets exported globally with great violence, is both valid and legitimate.

Ideas related to dignity, human, universality, are also evident outside of Western thought. Case in point. Grovogui (2011) distinguishes between the notions of the subject of rights in three declarations (French, U.S. and Haiti). For the French, the subject was the citizen, and the rules concerned the relationships between citizens and between the citizen and the government, with the rights that ensued from this relationship. In the American States, the individualistic subject wished to protect his rights from a government that he perceived as potentially encroaching on them. In both, the desire was to afford protection against government oppression. However, because in Haiti the slave had never enjoyed constitutional protection, the purpose of the constitution was to moralize what it meant to be human and to ensure what was needed to sustain life. Hence, it included within its provisions the illegitimate child, the orphan, the divorced and abandoned woman, and others normally excluded within its constitutional order. In contrast to the Enlightenment mistrust of unrestrained emotion as characteristic of those still living in a state of nature and needing to be educated to a state of reason, Haitian human rights relied on what Grovogui (2006) has elsewhere called the politics of the gut.

As such, Western human rights theory alone cannot account for the ways in which rights have been perceived and expressed globally. There are numerous local charters and documents which frame human rights within a particular local context, such as the African Commission on Human and Peoples' Rights, which in addition to protecting the "human" rights of the individual African, it also refers to collective "peoples'" rights.

I assert that the contents of a notion of human rights are not unchanging, but are rather subject to both historical and social contexts. That said, the existence of a variety of moral systems and of the ways in which they intersect, may provide an opportunity to expand the interpretation and the application of universal human rights. Here I rely on Mutua's (2002) book, *Human Rights: A Political and Cultural Critique*. I argue that whilst Mutua provides a cogent critique of the human rights enterprise that exposes both its Western ideological origins and its ongoing investment in a neo-colonialist mentality of saving the victims (and redeeming the savagery) of the global South, he ends up returning to the form of human rights—albeit a human rights framework suitably reconstructed so as to lead to a genuine, dialogic and cross-cultural universality. Mutua is ultimately led back to human rights as the proper modality in which his cross-cultural universality is to be realized. Human rights are hence redeemed not via resort to pragmatism but rather by the search for (another, truer) universality.

Mutua is both reconstructive in orientation and committed not only to the notion that a genuine universality is possible but also to the idea that the extant forms of the human rights regime, if cleansed of substantive Eurocentric bias, can yet still serve as the modality for a future universalism. The broadening and deepening of the universal consensus on the formulation and implementation of human rights takes place first within a given cultural formation and then across and beyond it, through processes of cross-cultural dialogue and exchange which seek to inform those within one culture of the normative bases adduced for human rights in other cultures and, in the process, to alter and expand those understandings.

The concept of rights is inherently paradoxical, aiming to achieve a utopian ideal, yet, often times, resorting to new forms of domination. Nonetheless, a human rights discourse, which seeks to protect the inherent dignity of each human being at all times and in all places, is a starting point for securing the linguistic dignity of our youth.

Methodology

This book began as a case study on three successful DLI schools in California. For 24 months, I conducted an extensive mixed-method study, managing over 42 individual interviews, 9 focus group interviews, alumni and parent surveys, coding narratives and letters, and scouring data, to illuminate the power and impact of DLI education for our youth. As the narratives of teachers, parents, students, and alumni took shape, I recognized commanding and unique perspectives on new possibilities for DLI education.

I switched gears. I focused my analysis on a new way to frame and consider the possibilities. As a result of the powerful voices and experiences on the ground, the relationship between linguistic human rights education and bilingual education began to unfold. Thus, the book is grounded in both qualitative data as well as theoretical work. In the following sections, I will detail the qualitative aspects of the work.

Narrative Inquiry

Narrative inquiry guided the qualitative methods employed for students, teachers, and parents. According to Marshall and Rossman (2016), narrative inquiry "values the signs, the symbols and the expressions of feelings in language and other symbol systems, validating how the narrator constructs meaning. It is especially effective when exploring issues of social change, causality, and social identity." As such, this is a qualitative study that assigned primal importance to how bilingual youth, bilingual teachers, and parents assigned meaning and experienced various aspects of DLI education.

It is important to note the dynamics of conducting research for and with youth, in this case bilingual youth. Children in school are difficult populations to study, because sadly schools have not traditionally been spaces for open dialogue and critical thinking. I often run into the issue of feeling the student is telling me what he/she thinks I want to hear.

For this reason, one of the most valuable types of research on youth is actually research about research. I firmly believe that the value of research is dependent on the way researchers go about conducting it. Methodology is critical. The better the methodology of the research, the truer the findings will be. Although I did not utilize youth participatory action research, a viable and relevant approach, I did take certain measures to ensure the students felt comfortable, safe, and that I was in fact capturing what they really wanted to say. Building trust with the students took much more time in comparison to the teachers and parents. I began with focus groups so students felt as though they were talking with each other, and not just with me. I could witness nodding heads as to whether or not an expressed idea was meaningful, noting this in my notebook to follow up with at a later point. I was also interested by what was not stated. I know from personal experience as a mother what my own boys struggle with and complain about in regard to school. Extracting these narratives often started with me sharing some of those stories.

Alongside the formal individual and focus group interviews, I made sure the students had access to me. I gave the students my cell number, and told them that if there was anything they wanted to communicate to me, they could text me. This was enormously effective. Students would text me questions, specific struggles with language and/or identity, hilarious anecdotes, or an interesting thought they came up with. These exchanges were followed up with conversation and note-taking.

Setting

The study took place at three DLI K-5 schools. Two of the schools are public-charters and one school is public. These schools are located in middle and lower middle-class neighbourhoods within large urban cities in Northern and Southern California respectively. These communities are racially and economically segregated. Unlike so many schools in the surrounding neighborhoods, the schools are integrated and highly diverse. Within the Latinx population, we find families from rural farming backgrounds in southern Mexico to middle class second and third generation Latinos who want their children to learn and speak Spanish. Despite racial/ethnic and linguistic diversity, there is a clear socioeconomic divide. Daughters and sons of cleaning ladies and restaurant workers mingle with the children of university professors.

The three DLI schools have been in operation for over 10 years. The California Association of Bilingual Education honored two of the schools with an Excellence Award.

Participants

Participants included bilingual youth, bilingual teachers, and parents. The participants in the study are diverse in age, race, sexual orientation, class background and ability. Participants were recruited at the school sites, starting with bilingual teachers who agreed to participate in the study and allowed me to observe in their classrooms. Snowballing allowed me to connect with parents who were interested in sharing their understandings and experiences with DLI education.

All bilingual youth ranged in age from 7–13, and were either currently enrolled or had graduated from a K-5 DLI school. They self-identified as Latina/o, White, African American, and bi/multiracial. There were notable contrasts vis-à-vis socio-economic background and experiences. Middle class White, Latina/o, and African American students were well-travelled, owned individual smartphones and tablets with internet access, and lived in single-family residences. Students from lower income backgrounds all self-identified as Latina/o or biracial, and travelled frequently to Mexico and Central America, lived in the poorer areas of the city comprised of mostly apartments and rental homes.

The bilingual teachers represented a more homogenous group. The majority of bilingual teachers, with the exception of 5, self-identified as Hispanic or Latina/o. All the teachers are fluent in both Spanish and English, and hold a BCLAD credential. All but two teachers possess a Master's Degree in Education. In addition, all but two teachers who participated in the study were women. The teachers' experience working in DLI classrooms ranged between 5 to 23 years.

The parents of bilingual youth were diverse in regard to race, class, and linguistic background. Parents self-identified as Latina/o, African American, and biracial. Ethnicity and immigrant status varied as well, with parents representing different nationalities as well as second and third generation identity markers. In light of gender, mothers comprised the majority of parents who agreed to participate in the study. In Northern California, 5 fathers who self-identify as gay/queer did participate in both individual and focus group interviews.

Interviews

In-depth interviews with bilingual youth, teachers, and parents consisted of three general areas: (1) knowledge and beliefs about bilingualism; (2) information on their experiences in DLI programs and schools, and (3) pedagogical insights on the teaching of languages and its impact. The interviews lasted between 30 minutes to two hours. The questions were guided by literature on bilingual education and the relationship among language, power, and identity.

Focus groups were conducted at the school sites with bilingual youth, bilingual teachers, and parents. I also asked bilingual youth and teachers to reflect upon their identity as biliterate human beings and their own experiences with language, culture, and power. The journal writing exercises spanned six months, providing a reflective space to record a variety of experiences. The teachers were much more receptive to the journaling exercises. Although I did receive a handful of thoughtful reflections from students, as stated previously, texting and group discussion were the preferred tool for communication.

Lastly, I relied on journal records, photographs, letters, autobiographical writing, email messages, and other data shared by the students, teachers and parents.

Participant Observation

I observed each school several times throughout the year for two years. I spent most of my time in the classroom, some days supporting the teacher with small group work. I walked around the playground during recesses, and observed the rituals of dropping off and picking up students before and after school. I attended two theatre performances, and four faculty meetings. I also attended one PTA meeting in the evening.

Data Analysis

The following steps were utilized in examining and analyzing the data: (a) organization and preparation of data included typed transcriptions from each interview (I eliminated youth overuse of "like" and "um" to ensure the flow of ideas for the reader. I also translated the Spanish interviews to English); detailed descriptions from observational field notes were typed and arranged by date and relevance; documents and audiovisual materials were arranged into initial categories; (b) overview of the data included initial perceptions captured through memoing and organizing data into large categories such as organization, beliefs, and actions; (c) coding the data was completed by hand on the initial transcripts and observational field notes; (d) identifying emerging themes, which were organized and arranged for member checking in a follow-up interview that was recorded, transcribed, and used to add description to the findings; (e) a qualitative narrative and learning map which were created to provide a detailed account and visual map of the findings; (f) interpretation and research findings with my own reflections on the research process were analyzed as a last step.

Real names and exact locations were not used in this study. Participants were given the option to change their mind on using their real names in the study at any point in the process. In order to protect the confidentiality of students, there is no identifiable information included in this study.

I cannot state strongly enough the importance of member checking to further maintain the integrity of the data. I selected a few narratives to review and analyze working themes. Participants confirmed that the themes resonated with their individual experiences. I incorporated their feedback into the final narrative (Marshall & Rossman, 2006). Thus, the data collection and analysis conformed to the highest standards of qualitative research, using the common qualitative tools and technologies of triangulation, member checks, thick descriptions and audit trails.

Overview of the Book

Part 1: Being Human, Being Bilingual—A Human Right to Language

Chapter 1: The Human Right to Language
This chapter provides an overview of how linguistic human rights came to be. The imposition of a single language on diverse groups living within a border can be traced back to 18th-century Spain, and the expansion and formation of modern European states. The language of the powerful was the dominant one, and was used to secure conformity within and expansion outside of the border. Thus, the ideology of one state, one nation, and one language was exported for the purpose of control and domination over all aspects of the colonized state. It was not until World War I and World War II, which involved the generation of Peace Treaties and multilateral and international conventions under the United Nations, that the protection of linguistic minorities encompassed broader and more far-reaching implications for nation state policies and practices. Presently, a platform of UN international declarations and conventions advocate (1) Mother tongue instruction as a means of improving educational quality by building on the knowledge and experience of the learners and teachers; (2) Bi/multilingual education at all levels of education as a means of promoting both social and gender equality, and as a key element of linguistically diverse societies; and (3) Language as an essential component of inter-cultural education to encourage understanding between different population groups and to ensure respect for fundamental rights.

Chapter 2: Language Rights in the United States
This chapter explores the possibilities of framing bilingual education as a human right. In the United States, courts, legislatures, policymakers, and even advocates all use a non-discrimination paradigm for addressing language right claims. This paradigm treats language as a trait that can inhibit the full exercise of rights and lead to harmful discrimination. It essentially sees language as a disadvantage for non-English speakers, which must be managed until it

can be overcome. Thus, language rights in the U.S. legal system are seen as guaranteeing the right to be free from discrimination on the basis of a lack of English fluency.

International human rights law represents a comprehensive body of jurisprudence that is unfamiliar and underutilized in the United States. Unites States law offers an impressive range of protections for the individual, but has its limitations with respect to the rights of linguistic minorities. International human rights law offers a more comprehensive approach to adjudicating language rights. By categorizing education as a human right, and within that, connecting language rights with culture, a human rights approach can inform U.S. policies on education for linguistic minorities.

This chapter concludes by positioning bilingual education within a human rights framework, moving beyond pedagogical effectiveness and capturing the deeper mantra that language is connected to humanity. Our youth possess fundamental human rights, including linguistic rights. To deny bilingual education to our students is to deny their rights as human beings. This choice of employing a human rights vocabulary serves a fairly specific function: it endows a language claim with unconditional normative value and immediate applicability irrespective of local context. Louis Henkin, widely considered one of the most influential human rights scholars of the 20th century, writes that "human rights enjoy a prima facie, a presumptive inviolability." According to Henkin, human rights are "universal," in the dual sense that they are (i) widely recognized and "the only political-moral idea that has received universal acceptance," and (ii) that they impose external standards on states that "apply to all to whom they are relevant," across "geography or history, culture or ideology, political or economic system, or stages of societal development."

Thus, the power of linguistic human rights lies in their universal properties. Bi/plurilingual education is tethered to our students' humanity and their inalienable rights as human beings to live and learn their mother tongue.

Chapter 3: Bilingual Education as a Human Right

This chapter provides an in-depth analysis of DLI education in the United States. In its conception, DLI discourse emphasized concepts such as human dignity, inter-culturalism, and peace. As English-Only and NCLB policies permeated classroom practices, researchers in the field of bilingual education focused their attention towards the effectiveness of bilingual education— that is, in arguing that bilingual education is good because it works. Bilingual education research tends to argue and reargue, cite and recite, its pedagogical effectiveness to make the case for countering English-only education.

Moreover, DLI guidelines emphasize inter-culturalism as an additional benefit of bilingual educational, though research and discourse surrounding inter-culturalism rarely address issues such as race and power (i.e., white supremacy).

Recent scholarship on DLI education point to the push for constructing bilingual education programs on shaky foundations and fail to provide their teachers with adequate training—compromising the success of dual language programs before they even begin. In addition to this, the asymmetry we find in dual language program instruction, resources, and students (problematically favoring English over the partner language) makes it difficult to adequately collect data, as issues of power and language permeate the establishment and execution of these programs.

In the Unites States, neoliberal and global capital ideologies have troublingly taken precedence over quality and care in education policy and implementation, leaving us with pedagogical models that fail to view learning and students as ends in and of themselves. To view students as sources of capital—that is, as a *means* to measurable ends—is to dehumanize education, favoring quantity and production over quality and human dignity, and ultimately distancing educators from the humanity of their students.

The most significant challenge for DLI programs and schools will be to protect and deepen a commitment to linguistic human rights from neoliberal and global capital assaults.

Part 2: A Humanizing Dual Language Immersion Education

Children have a fundamental human right to learn in their mother tongue(s). Access to the learning of language, particularly the language of culture and connection, is vital to one's humanity. This central focus on humanness is what brings me to the potential of framing the education of learning languages, in this case bilingual education, under a human rights framework.

I posit an alternative framework to challenge the more traditional work in DLI education. Parallels between traditional schooling and DLI education are drawn through an examination of human capital theory, a framework with substantial currency in traditional education. Human capital theory contends that a valuable education is that which increases students' contribution in the global economic market. In addition, human capital theory transforms teaching and learning into systems that can be standardized and quantified. Student performance is rarely measured beyond a standardized score. In spite of the growing body of research evidencing the harm and profitability of one-size-fits-all standards and high stakes testing, DLI schools are increasingly succumbing to the pressure.

Three principles—*Intentionality, Sustenance, Imaginings*—frame the final three chapters of the book. I interweave classroom observations, interviews, written reflections, and stories from those who live and breathe bilingual education—our bilingual youth, teachers, and parents. I evidence the powerful work that already exists to connect our language to our humanity. In the end, a humanizing DLI education is anchored in the epistemology of bilingual youth. Their ways of knowing must inform what and how we teach. In this way, a DLI education hears their language(s) and feels their humanity.

Note

1   Recognizing that labels problematically categorize individuals and deny their rich experiences and identities, I use the term minoritized, to indicate racial, ethnic, or linguistic groups that may be labeled minority by whitestream society (Urrieta, 2010) but who are by no means "minor."

PART 1

Being Human, Being Bilingual—A Human Right to Language

∵

CHAPTER 1

Language as a Human Right

Human rights are intrinsic to being human—inherent to all individuals—and are fundamental, inalienable, and inviolable (Skutnabb-Kangas, 2000). Echoing the United Nations Office of the High Commissioner for Human Rights' (OHCNR) definition of human rights, human rights apply to every individual without discrimination regarding gender, race, ethnicity, culture, residence, language, and so on. These rights are typically expressed through international laws in the form of treaties, customary international laws, or general principles, binding participating governments to engage in and refrain from certain actions in order to protect and promote basic human rights, as well as the freedom of individuals and groups (www.ohchr.org).

Human rights have been at the center of politics at all levels—studied, discussed, and clarified at research institutions among international lawyers, philosophers, and experts in various fields. Despite various declarations to promote linguistic diversity, linguistic human rights have been absent from binding international human rights instruments, especially those pertaining to education, which has resulted in other human attributes receiving more attention (Skutnabb-Kangas, 2000). Over time, however, language rights have been integrated into human rights as 'linguistic human rights'—a concept that has required cooperation among experts from various fields.

Human Rights and Language

According to Illich (1981), the imposition of a single language on diverse groups living within a border can be traced back to 18th-century Spain, and the expansion and formation of modern European states. The language of the powerful was the dominant one, and was used to secure conformity within and expansion outside the border. Thus, the ideology of one state, one nation, and one language was exported for the purpose of control and domination over all aspects of the colonized state (Skutnabb-Kangas, 2000).

In modern history, the United Nations played and continues to play an instrumental role in defining and protecting language rights in relation to minority rights. It should be noted that national initiatives have also played a significant role in addressing language rights, such as Article 19 from the Austrian Constitutional Law of 1867, which states:

© KONINKLIJKE BRILL NV, LEIDEN, 2019 | DOI:10.1163/9789004389724_001

> All the ethnic minorities of the State shall enjoy the same rights and, in particular, have an absolute right to maintain and develop their nationality and their language. All the languages used in the provinces are recognized by the State as having equal rights with regard to education, administration and public life. In provinces inhabited by several ethnic groups, the public educational institutions shall be organized in such a way as to enable all ethnic groups to acquire the education they need in their own language, without being obliged to learn another language of the province. (Capotoxrti, 1979, p. 3)

Nonetheless, it was not until World War I and World War II, which involved the generation of Peace Treaties and multilateral and international conventions under the League of Nations (later replaced by the United Nations), that clauses were included to protect linguistic minorities in a broader and more far-reaching manner. This was first felt in Central and Eastern Europe (Capotorti, 1979). Interestingly enough, nations such as Britain, France, and the United States—signatories to the minorities' treaties—did not extend linguistic rights to minorities at home. Skutnabb-Kangas (2000) argues that this illustrates how slow the process of implementation is, as many linguistic minorities all over the world are still without sufficient linguistic rights, despite the fact that their respective countries are signatories on international human rights treaties.

Another significant development worth highlighting is the role that decolonization played in the development of collective rights (versus the Western emphasis on individual rights). This has particular implications for linguistic minorities in that it ultimately led to a more complicated understanding of how language, culture, and identity are inextricably linked. UN documents ensured the cultural characteristics of minorities were adequately covered in reference to ethnic, religious, and linguistic minorities.

According to Skutnabb-Kangas (2000), after World War II, language became one of the key characteristics protected from discrimination in the preliminary statements and general clauses of many multilateral, regional, and international documents, including: Article 1 in the Universal Declaration of Human Rights; Article 2.1 in the International Covenant on Civil and Political Rights; Article 2.2 in the International Covenant on Economic, Social and Cultural Rights; Article 1 in the American Convention on Human Rights; Article 2.1 in the United Nations Convention on the Right of the Child; Article 1 in the United Nations International Convention on the Protection of the Rights of All Migrant Workers and Members of Their Families; and Article 13 in the Charter of the United Nations. However, when one looks deeply at binding clauses of these documents, especially those that pertain to education, there appears to be a change in position, as language is suddenly not present. Language rights disappear in educational clauses in documents such as the Universal Declaration of Human Rights (1948) and the International Covenant on Economic, Social and Cultural Rights (adopted in 1966), in which the paragraphs dealing with education include only race, ethnicity, and religion (Skutnabb-Kangas, 2000).

Where Are We Now?

International human rights law takes a culture-based approach to language rights, recognizing that language and cultural identity are inextricably intertwined. The culture-based approach to language rights in international human rights law has three basic prongs. First, language rights ensure fair and proper treatment of traditionally repressed minorities so as to remove potential sources of conflict in multiethnic societies. Second, language rights intend to guarantee the civil rights of individuals, acknowledging the possibility of discrimination on the basis of language, as well as the reality that general rights may be uniquely denied to language minorities. Third, language rights seek to guarantee diversity and promote the existence and flourishing of multiple cultural identities within a given society. Human rights instruments thus guarantee language rights as a means of protecting the development of cultural identity, "enriching the fabric of society as a whole." Demanding the promotion of language diversity, diverse identities, and multiculturalism, the international human rights law approach emphatically rejects obligatory assimilation.

While there is no international human rights treaty dedicated solely to language rights, multiple international human rights norms closely connect language rights with culture. These norms establish broad obligations to protect and promote the languages and cultural identities of minority language speakers. Two of the main UN human rights treaties—the International Covenant on Civil and Political Rights (ICCPR) 48 and the Convention on the Rights of the Child (CRC)—explicitly link language and cultural identity. The ICCPR and the CRC are particularly important in understanding this approach, because the two treaties are among the most widely ratified human rights instruments in the world. Article 27 of the ICCPR, mirrored in Article 30 of the CRC, states:

> [P]ersons belonging to [ethnic, linguistic, or religious] minorities shall not be denied the right, in community with other members of their group, to enjoy their own culture, to profess and practice their own religion, or to use their own language.

The UN body charged with interpreting the International Covenant on Economic, Social and Cultural Rights recently laid out the connection between non-discrimination provisions, language, and culture. In its General Comment No. 20 on Non-Discrimination, the Committee on Economic, Social and Cultural Rights notes: "[l]anguage barriers can hinder the enjoyment of many Covenant rights, including the right to participate in cultural life." Similarly, in Lopez-Alvarez v. Honduras, the Inter-American Court of Human Rights found a violation of equal protection with cultural identity when the Honduran State jailed a Garifuna minority rights activist, and inhibited him from using the Garifuna language in jail. The Court took pains to stress that one's "mother tongue represents an element of identity."

Linguistic Human Rights in Education

The UN Convention on the Rights of the Child (1990) draws a direct connection among education, language, and culture. Except for the United States and Somalia, all of the countries in the world have agreed to it. The first paragraph of Article 28 in the crc emphasizes that State Parties recognize the right of the child to education. The paragraph then proceeds to specify that State Parties shall "take measures to encourage regular attendance at schools and the reduction of drop-out rights." The first paragraph of Article 29 of the CRC similarly stresses, "The education of the child shall be directed to the development of the child's personality, talents and mental and physical abilities to their fullest potential ... to the development of respect for the child's parents, his or her own cultural identity, language and values, for the national values of the country in which the child is living, the country from which he or she may originate ...."

UNESCO's Mandate for Cultural and Linguistic Diversity in Education

In 2003, UNESCO mandated a strong commitment to quality education for all, and to cultural and linguistic diversity in education in Education in a Multilingual World (UNESCO Education Position Paper). Through subsequent position papers, policy briefs, and research reports, UNESCO continues to advocate for multilingualism in schools and contest monolingualism. In its report, 'Strong Foundations: Early Childhood Care and Education,' UNESCO (2007) points out the overlooked advantages of multilingual education in the early years. When children are offered opportunities to learn in their mother tongue, they are more likely to enroll and succeed in school (Kosonen, 2005) and their parents are more likely to communicate with teachers and participate in their children's learning (Benson, 2002).

Increasingly, cultural groups are realizing the need to ensure the transmission of their linguistic heritage to the youngest members of their communities. A compendium of examples produced by UNESCO (2008) attests to the resurgence of international interest in promoting mother tongue-based education, and to the wide variety of models, tools, and resources now being developed and tested to promote learning programs in the mother tongue. Moreover, a platform of international declarations and conventions support the learning of at least two languages in education: a mother tongue and a language of the larger community, as well as access to international languages. In Education in a Multilingual World (2003), UNESCO espouses:

1. Mother tongue instruction as a means of improving educational quality by building on the knowledge and experience of the learners and teachers;
2. Bi/multilingual education at all levels of education as a means of promoting both social and gender equality and as a key element of linguistically diverse societies;
3. Language as an essential component of inter-cultural education to encourage understanding between different population groups and ensure respect for fundamental rights.

Thus, in regard to education, the linguistic rights that have been framed in international agreements for minority and indigenous groups include the following: schooling in their languages, if so desired; access to the language of the larger community and to that of national education systems; inter-cultural education that promotes positive attitudes to minority and Indigenous languages and the cultures they express; and access to international languages.

It is important to note that UNESCO stresses multilingual education (in lieu of bilingual education). UNESCO adopted the term 'multilingual education' in 1999 in the General Conference Resolution 12 to refer to the use of at least three languages: L1, a regional or national language, and an international language in education. The resolution supported the view that the requirements of global and national participation and the specific needs of particular, culturally and linguistically distinct communities can only be addressed by multilingual education. In regions where the language of the learner is not the official or national language of the country, bi/multilingual education can make mother tongue instruction possible while providing at the same time the acquisition of languages used in larger areas of the country and the world. This additive approach to bilingualism is different from the so-called subtractive bilingualism that aims to move children on to a second language as the language of instruction.

Conclusion

In conclusion, although there have been efforts to promote linguistic diversity, and it has been recognized as a crucial dimension of human rights discourse, linguistic human rights is yet to become a prominent aspect of binding international human right instruments—especially those pertaining to education. 'Linguistic human rights' is itself a relatively new concept, one that recognizes that language and cultural identity are inextricably intertwined and fundamental to our sense of who we are.

Beyond this, education (and our basic human right to education) is vital to the understanding and enrichment of our cultural identity, and properly fostering the mother tongue *in education*—that is, opting for additive, rather than subtractive bi/multilingualism—is a crucial dimension of this process. With this, we can turn to the history of language rights in the United States, and its relation to bi/multilingual education.

CHAPTER 2

Language Rights in the United States

This chapter explores the possibilities of framing bilingual education within a human rights discourse. In the United States, courts, legislatures, policymakers, and even advocates all use a non-discrimination paradigm for addressing language right claims. This paradigm treats language as a trait that can inhibit the full exercise of rights and lead to harmful discrimination. It essentially sees language as a disadvantage for non-English speakers, which must be managed until it can be overcome. Thus, language rights in the U.S. legal system are seen as guaranteeing the right to be free from discrimination on the basis of a lack of English fluency.

International human rights law represents a comprehensive body of jurisprudence that is unfamiliar and underutilized in the United States. Unites States law offers an impressive range of protections for the individual, but has its limitations with respect to the rights of linguistic minorities. International human rights law offers a more comprehensive approach to adjudicating language rights. By categorizing education as a human right, and within that, connecting language rights with culture, a human rights approach can inform U.S. policy on education for linguistic minorities. This chapter explores the basis for, and possibilities of, language rights under international human rights law, concluding with the central assertion that if education is a human right, then bilingual education is a means to that end.

The U.S. Approach to Language Rights

The United States has no official language, and generally leaves decisions about the language of instruction to states, district, and schools. Federal law does, however, affirm the rights of Native American populations—including American Indians, Alaska Natives, Native Hawaiians, and Pacific Islanders—to use and develop their native languages. The Native American Languages Act (NALA) of 1990 asserts that it is U.S. policy to: "preserve, protect, and promote the rights and freedoms of Native Americans to use, practice, and develop Native American languages"; encourage and support the use of Native American languages as a medium of instruction; encourage institutions of elementary, secondary, and higher education, where appropriate, to include Native American languages in the curriculum in a manner comparable to other

© KONINKLIJKE BRILL NV, LEIDEN, 2019 | DOI:10.1163/9789004389724_002

world languages; and allow exceptions to teacher qualification requirements for federal programs in situations where the requirements inhibit the employment of teachers who can teach in a Native American language (NALA, 25 U.S.C. 2903).

The U.S. legal system aims to guarantee the right to be free from discrimination on the basis on English fluency, and therefore employs a non-discrimination paradigm when addressing language rights claims. Language is thus recognized as a characteristic that can be used to inhibit the free exercise of human rights in the same way that gender, race, ethnicity, or culture can be used to discriminate against non-majority community members. Most legal debates on language rights involve claims about national origin discrimination. Case law analyzes language claims as forms of national origin discrimination under the Equal Protection Clause to the United States Constitution or, even more frequently, under the provisions of the Civil Rights Act of 1964, which prohibits discrimination in housing, employment, and in federally funded programs. Some case law applies state and local anti-discrimination constitutional or statutory provisions. As a result, advocacy and policymaking revolves around conceptions of non-discrimination.

The use of non-discrimination principles is prevalent across the range of contexts in which language rights claims arise. For instance, courts look to the provisions of the Civil Rights Act, as well as parallel state and local laws prohibiting discrimination to determine the legality of English Only workplace rules. The same provisions are used to address refusals to hire non-English speakers without an objective basis in job qualifications. These provisions have also served as the basis for courts to strike down differential treatment in the workplace because of someone who appears to have a foreign accent. Policymakers and advocates also look to discrimination standards in the context of interactions between the government and non-English speakers. They have argued that interpretation and translation services must be provided to ensure that the government provides access to non-English speakers without discrimination.

In the case of education, the issue of minority language speakers in schools is primarily addressed through the lens of statutory non-discrimination provisions. The seminal decision of the United States Supreme Court in Lau v. Nichols applied the Civil Rights Act to find discrimination on the basis of national origin where non-English speaking children could not equally participate in education because it was only provided in English. That case and the Equal Educational Opportunities Act of 1974, following in its wake, continue to frame much of the debate about bilingual education.

While the United States Supreme Court concedes that the equal protection clause does apply to language in the context of education, it has not gone anywhere near as far as international human rights law. If linguistic minorities are to survive in countries in which a variety of languages are spoken, it is vital that the various languages be used in the school system, especially at the primary level, since language is inextricably connected with education. As described in the previous chapter, recent UNESCO proclamations affirm the necessity of mother tongue education as a means to the human right to education, among others. Educational systems should therefore be responsible for language-minority-children's multilingual development because it is necessary for participation in society. Unless educational institutions have the appropriate staffing to provide an equal education for multilingual children, the language minority will inevitably face language loss, as children are forcibly transferred to the language majority by way of monolingual education.

The Dismantling of Bilingual Rights and Education in the United States

bell hooks writes: "I know that it is not the English language that hurts me, but what oppressors do with it, how they shape it to become a territory that limits and defines, how they make it a weapon that can shame, humiliate, colonize" (hooks, 1994). As hooks highlights, language cannot be understood outside of the context of power. Within spoken language is the capacity to both liberate and oppress, to control and to free.

The move towards English Only classrooms in the United States situates bilingual education within a larger contestation of power in relation to the education of our nation's ever-growing linguistic minority populations. For much of the 20th century, public schools enforced monolingual education, excluding and prohibiting the use of languages other than English in school. For instance, in the case of Spanish and Mexican-American children, these forms of discrimination derive from a vision of the language and culture of Mexican-American children as representing a "foreign element" that needed "Americanizing." Proponents of legislation designating English as the official language of the United States have adopted a tone that is openly critical of specific national origin groups, particularly Latinx. For example, Senator S. I. Hayakawa, who was one of the founders and most vocal proponents of the movement, claimed that the "aggressive movement on the part of Hispanics … to reject assimilation and to seek and maintain … a foreign language within our borders is an unhealthy development."

Given this history of targeting non-English languages and cultures, it is not surprising that the connections between language and culture continue to motivate negative reactions to minority language use. These reactions are based on biases against languages spoken by specific national origin groups, as well as presumptions relating to the culture and identity of those groups. As linguistic diversity in our nation continues to grow, the U.S. Census Bureau estimates about 20 percent of the school-age population speaks a language other than English at home (Gándara & Hopkins, p. xiii). It is imperative that we understand that the conversations surrounding bilingual education are shaped by larger political debates and power struggles in recent decades. Gains made during the Civil Rights era have been usurped as new waves of "conservatism, neoliberalism, assimilationism, and xenophia" emerge, representing a larger move to English Only policies in our schools (Gándara & Hopkins, 2010).

Federal and State Policies in Language Education

Landmark legislation from the 1960s and 1970s, such as Lau vs. Nichols, in which the Supreme Court affirmed the right of non-English speaking students to an education equal to that of their English speaking peers, and subsequently, the Bilingual Education Act and Title VII of the Elementary and Secondary Education Act, established the necessity and agency for schools to provide instruction in a student's native language, most frequently Spanish. The ambiguity of the legislation, however, on what the intention of bilingual education was to be—be it to develop other languages, or to move to English as quickly as possible—sowed the seeds for controversy and struggles for power in the decades that followed (Gándara et al., 2004).

In 2001, with the passing of the No Child Left Behind Act under the Bush administration, the word "bilingual" was completely removed from the legislation. Moreover, what was formerly known as the "Office of Bilingual Education and Minority Language Affairs" within the Department of Education instead became the "Office of English Language Acquisition, Language Enhancement, and Academic Achievement for Limited-English Proficient Students." Moreover, "The National Clearinghouse for Bilingual Education" also became the "the National Clearinghouse for English Language Acquisition and Language Instruction Education Programs." As our borders tightened in the wake of September 11, 2001, and the political climate became increasingly hostile to "Other" ethnicities, our treatment of "Other" languages has also become increasingly intolerant.

After 2001, the intention of language education became clear: teach students English. Valuing a student's home language and culture or promoting biliteracy were clearly not the goals; assimilation and the promotion of a unified national identity around the English language were embraced. Describing the history of the implementation of bilingual education laznguage programs in the U.S., Gándara and Contreras (2009) write:

It was not to be implemented for any of the other possible goals that a bilingual education program might have, such as achieving literacy in the primary language or strengthening student's disciplinary knowledge. This narrow construction of language competence has led many schools to back away from using primary language instruction that can strengthen student's general academic skills. (p. 127)

At the state level, the implementation and development of bilingual education programs has been ripe with controversy, politicization, and widespread opposition. Opponents of bilingual education and immigrant rights have sought to dismantle primary language instruction throughout the country, and have been successful in fostering an English Only movement in many states. Anti-bilingual education measures have been successful in states such as California and Massachusetts—states comprised of large immigrant populations.

The Case of California

As a destination for refugees, agrarian workers, and immigrants from areas including Mexico, Central America, and Asia, many non-English speakers live in California. Principal linguistic minorities in California include Latinx, Chinese, and Vietnamese.

In 1986, California voters overwhelmingly passed an initiative that amended the state constitution to declare English as the state's official language. Proposition 63's stated purpose is to "preserve, protect and strengthen" the English language. California's English Only amendment requires that the legislature "take all steps necessary to insure that the role of English as the common language of the State of California is preserved and enhanced." No law that "diminishes or ignores the role of English as the common language" can be passed, and the amendment is "not to supersede any of the rights guaranteed" by the state constitution.

Most vulnerable to attack under this amendment were bilingual public education, multilingual ballots, multilingual emergency services, and information concerning public benefits. In Guiterrez v. Municipal Court of the South-East Judicial District, a Los Angeles Municipal Court promulgated a rule requiring court employees to speak only English in court offices, unless the employees were translating for the public or on a lunch break. Guiterrez, a bilingual Hispanic-American employed as deputy court clerk, challenged this rule. One of her duties as a clerk was to translate for the Spanish speaking public.

While the Ninth Circuit Court of Appeals in Guiterrez v. Municipal Court of the South-East Judicial District discussed the California English Only amendment, the court did not reach the amendment's validity under the equal protection clause. The Ninth Circuit ultimately rejected the appellant's argument that the Los Angeles Court's rule was required by California's English Only amendment. The court reasoned that the California Constitution simply asserts that English is the state's official language, and does not require that English be the only language spoken. The court rejected the contention that all government communications be in English, since the official use of Spanish was permitted (and sometimes mandated) for official business. In addition, the Ninth Circuit held that even though an individual may be bilingual, "his primary language remains an important link to his ethnic culture and identity." While Guiterrez contains helpful reasoning concerning the importance of language to group identity, the decision sheds no light on equal protection issues arising out of English Only imperatives.

In Guadalupe Organization, Inc. v. Tempe Elementary School District No.3, public elementary school children of Mexican-American and Native American (Yaqui) descent brought suit against their school district to insist that it provide bilingual and bicultural education for the non-English-speaking students. The United States Court of Appeals for the Ninth Circuit applied the rational basis test to the claim. Citing San Antonio Independent School District v. Rodriguez, the Ninth Circuit reasoned that while bilingual education is an important interest, it is not a fundamental right guaranteed by the Constitution. The Guadalupe court concluded that the equal protection clause does not require the state to provide bicultural or bilingual education. The court further held that the school district met its constitutional obligations by adopting measures "to cure existing language deficiencies of non-English-speaking students."

According to the Guadalupe court, the school's program did not "fail 'to provide each child with an opportunity to acquire the basic minimal skills necessary for the enjoyment of rights of speech and of full participation in the political process.'" The court asserted that linguistic and cultural diversity, despite their occasional advantages, are actually detrimental to a nation, and concluded that bilingual and bicultural education are issues to be decided on a local level, and are neither mandated nor prohibited by the Constitution.

Proposition 227

The passing of Proposition 227 in California serves as a window through which we can understand the movement towards English Only education in the United States. Introduced in 1998 by a Silicon Valley entrepreneur Ron Unz, the ballot, requiring English to be the language of instruction, passed with a surprising 61 percent of the vote, defeated only in Alameda and San Francisco counties. Successful anti-bilingual education measures in Arizona and Massachusetts followed suit. Despite the fact that research overwhelmingly confirms that instruction in one's native language results in better outcomes in literacy in English, and does not impede on language learners' achievement in English, Unz's measure framed bilingual education as a waste of taxpayer dollars, and blamed bilingual education for the achievement gap between Latinx students and English learners, and non-Latinx students and English speakers (Contreras & Gándara, 2009).

Proposition 58

In 2016, Proposition 58 repealed the English-only immersion requirement and waiver provisions required by Proposition 227, which dictated that English learners were to take one year of intensive English instruction before transitioning to English-only classes. Proposition 58 no longer required English Only education for English learners; it allowed schools to utilize multiple programs, including bilingual education programs, in which students learn from teachers who speak both their native language and English. It also made parental waivers no longer necessary to take non-English-only classes. If requested by enough parents, the measure requires schools to offer specific English learner programs. Furthermore, the measure instated that school districts and county offices of education must ask for annual feedback on English learner programs from parents and community members.

What is worth noting is that despite Proposition 58's repeal of waiver provisions required by Proposition 227, the primacy of learning English remains intact. English still needs to be at the center of educational objectives if bi/multilingual measures are to be accepted. Proposition 58 preserves the requirement that public schools are to ensure that students obtain English language proficiency, necessitating instruction that will "ensure English acquisition as rapidly and effectively as possible."

That said, school districts now have full authorization to establish dual-language immersion programs for both native and non-native English speakers. What we cannot ignore is that against the backdrop of increasing access to dli, language and power are still at play.

Building the Bridge: Bilingual Education and Linguistic Human Rights in the United States

Positioning bilingual education under a human rights framework allows us to address the basic right of our bi/multilingual youth to embrace their mother tongue as a vital dimension of their human dignity. Given the centrality of language to self-identification, to our sense of who we are, and our understanding of where we fit in the broader world, it is interesting that a connection between linguistic human rights and bilingual education has taken so long to emerge the dominant discourse for bi/multilingual education.

A human rights approach to language supports what is widely accepted as "the preeminent human rights norm": the ideal of nurturing cultural diversity at large. Henry Steiner, a leading human rights scholar, explains:

> By valuing diverse cultural traditions ... human rights law evidences what must be a basic assumption—namely that differences enrich ... the world. They contribute to a fund of human experience on which all individuals and groups can draw in the ongoing processes of change and growth.

By attributing so much importance to the intrinsic value of linguistic diversity—and to all of the benefits its promotion may bring—it implies that language rights are so important that they can qualify as nothing less than human rights. Language rights are human rights. Language rights constitute one of the most basic rights all human beings can claim and they cannot be compromised or negotiated; language is the fundamental way in which we understand each other, the world, and ourselves. Being bi/multilingual is thus a way of being human, a way that deserves protection.

The safeguarding of linguistic diversity is so important that it is simply not enough to indirectly protect linguistic rights through non-discrimination. They need to be guaranteed as positive rights. According to this approach, an ideal implementation of 'linguistic human rights' would require the states to guarantee these rights and public institutions to shoulder the burden of adjusting themselves to the linguistic diversity of the society.

Using a human rights vocabulary to regulate matters bearing on language serves a fairly specific function: it endows a language claim with unconditional normative value and immediate applicability irrespective of local context. Louis Henkin, widely considered one of the most influential human rights scholars of the 20th century, writes that "human rights enjoy a prima facie, a presumptive inviolability. The power of language rights lies in their "universal" properties. According to Henkin, human rights are "universal," in the dual sense that they are (i) widely recognized and "the only political-moral idea that has received universal acceptance" and (ii) that they impose external standards on states that "apply to all to whom they are relevant" across "geography or history, culture or ideology, political or economic system, or stages of societal development."

Linguistic human rights affirm that the protection of minorities' languages is closely associated with culture. Fernand de Varennes, a leading legal expert on language rights, explains that the "importance of language for many minorities" derives from the centrality of language "to their social and cultural identity." He notes that "the use of a particular language not only serves as a means of functional communication, but also expresses that person's cultural identity as well as the cultural heritage developed by all previous speakers of the language."

Important human rights legal instruments echo the notion that language is constitutive of culture: "Language is one of the most fundamental components of human identity. Hence, respect for a person's dignity is intimately connected with respect for the person's identity and consequently for the person's language." It is this language—emphasizing the relationship among language, culture, and humanity—that is starkly missing in research surrounding DLI. Although there are references to "inter-cultural competence," the argument that denying mother tongue education to linguistic minorities is a form of linguistic and cultural genocide seems to be quieter than the argument that bilingual education breeds interculturalism for all groups. A sort of, "we can all get along."

Conclusion

Questions of linguistic human rights are ultimately questions of language policy, and reflect underlying assumptions about the nature of language, as well as issues of power, equality, and access in society. As James Tollefson notes:

> The policy of requiring everyone to learn a single dominant language is widely seen as a common-sense solution to the communication problems of multilingual societies. The appeal of this assumption is such that monolingualism is seen as a solution to linguistic inequality. If linguistic minorities learn the dominant languages, so the argument goes, then they will not suffer economic and social inequality. The assumption is an example of an ideology which refers to normally unconscious assumptions that come to be seen as common sense ... such assumptions justify exclusionary policies and sustain inequality. (1991, p. 10)

This political narrative about the English Only movement cannot be understood apart from struggles for political power in our country. As Gándara and Contreras stress in *The Latino Education Crisis: The Consequences of Failed*

Social Policies, it is ultimately a question of "belonginess." "If one's language is accepted, there is a tacit understanding that the speaker of the language is also accepted" (Gándara & Contreras, 2009). The move towards English Only represents an attempt to maintain unequal power relations in society as a whole: an attempt to deny human rights.

Bilingual Education as a Human Right: The Case of Dual Language Immersion Education

In conclusion, quiero decir that these changes scare me. Returning to la mujer scares me, re-learning Spanish scares me. I have not spoken much of la lengua here. It is not so much that I have been avoiding it, only that the conclusion brings me to the most current point in time: la lengua.

In returning to the love of my race, I must return to the fact that not only has the mother been taken from me, but her tongue, her mothertongue. I want the language; feel my tongue rise to the occasion of feeling at home, in common. I know this language in my bones ... and then it escapes me ... "You don't belong. Quitate!"

CHERRIE MORAGA

∴

According to U.S. Department of Education statistics for 2012–2013, the number of students classified as "English learners" is approaching five million, which represents 4.2 percent growth since 2007–2008. Although a large majority of language learners come from Spanish-speaking homes, many other languages also are represented, including Vietnamese, Chinese, Arabic, Hmong, Bengali, Korean, Navajo, Nepali, Portuguese, and Somali, to mention just a few.

In this chapter, I analyze DLI education in the United States. Originally, DLI scholarship emphasized concepts such as human dignity, interculturalism, and peace. Once No Child Left Behind and English Only policies emerged, researchers in the field of bilingual education focused more of their attention on the *effectiveness* of bilingual education—that is, in arguing that bilingual education is good because it works. Scholarship for bilingual education thus tends to argue and reargue, cite and recite, its pedagogical effectiveness to make the case for countering English Only education. I posit that advocating for bilingual education from a human rights perspective moves beyond pedagogical effectiveness, and captures the larger mantra that language is connected to humanity. To deny bilingual education to our students is to deny their rights as human beings.

© KONINKLIJKE BRILL NV, LEIDEN, 2019 | DOI:10.1163/9789004389724_003

Being Bilingual, Being Human

When we acknowledge that language, culture, and identity are inextricably intertwined—that language and humanity are in fact connected—the consequences of establishing English as the dominant language are far-reaching. For instance, the loss of language weakens the possibility for finding solutions/wisdom through alternate linguistic thought patterns. Moreover, language minority students may experience shame, inner struggle, and identity crises. The systematic denial of linguistic rights is nothing short of a dehumanizing process for our language learners.

Exploring Configurations of "Human"

It has been argued that racial identities were imagined, categorized and employed to reflect notions of a normalized, Eurocentric White human (Fanon, 1967; Anzaldúa, 1987; Morrison, 1992; Mills, 1997). Post-structural Caribbean theorist Sylvia Wynter (1979) asserts that Whiteness had become the normalized constitution of culture "in relation to which all other cultures had been made subservient (p. 150). Wynter contends that the configuration of the human, then, operates within a cultural framework in which whiteness is considered to be more civilized and intelligent, and therefore more "human." This "quintessential, rational human" can be traced to the 18th century White, Protestant, European heterosexual male—who was constitutively and epistemologically dependent upon its ontological counterpart: *the other/the irrational/the inhuman* (Wynter, 1992; Ani, 1994). Thus, within this problematic system of thought, any person who does not exist within these structures—any person who is not White, Protestant, European heterosexual male—is also not fully human.

The construction of the ontologically "inhumane" other has significant implications in schooling contexts. Within educational and legal research, scholars have examined how the bodies of nonwhite students are not only perceived as abnormal, but are also oppressed, punished, criminalized, and exploited for this supposed abnormality, thus 'requiring' particular, and often, deficit-based, discriminatory interventions (Hanson, 2005; Alexander, 2012; Brown, 2013).

In other words, many students of color—and in our case, linguistic minoritized youth—experience a subtractive schooling process in American public schools in which students are and *feel* marginalized, excluded, and dehumanized in ways that do not support their full capacities (Valenzuela, 1999; Irvine, 2000; Noguera, 2003).

Dehumanizing Impact of English-Only

As argued previously, research increasingly shows that children's ability to learn a second or additional language (e.g., a lingua franca and an international language) does not suffer when their mother tongue is the primary language of instruction throughout primary school. Fluency and literacy in the mother tongue lay a cognitive and linguistic foundation for learning additional languages. When children receive formal instruction in their first language throughout primary school, and then gradually transition to academic learning in the second language, they learn the second language quickly. If they continue to have opportunities to develop their first language skills in secondary school, they emerge as fully bilingual (or multilingual) learners.

If, however, children are forced to switch abruptly or transition too soon from learning in their mother tongue to schooling in a second language, their first language acquisition may be attenuated or even lost. Even more importantly, their self-confidence as learners and their interest in what they are learning may decline, leading to lack of motivation, school failure, and early school leaving. As they approach textbooks, curricula, pedagogy devoid of their cultural and linguistic backgrounds, questions such as *do I exist?* And *do I have to cut off a part of my life?* lead children to a deep sense of alienation.

Even more dehumanizing, monolingual education destroys cultural and linguistic ties. In her research on language and family relations, Lily Wong-Filmore (1991) has found that English Only policies negatively affect many families. For young children, this is problematic and disastrous. When a child can no longer speak to her parents in the home language, the passing of cultural knowledge, values, and wisdom becomes truncated (Ada, 1993). More importantly, the loss of language weakens the possibility for finding solutions/ wisdom through alternative linguistic thought patterns.

Although linguistic and cultural hegemony has been a reality for many individuals and groups, it has not been totally successful, as the intensity of ethnic revival and attempts to reverse language shift demonstrate. The struggle to understand and save language forms is a quiet revolution to humanize. Cultural and linguistic impositions are not static. They are constantly renewed, contested, and negotiated.

The History of Dual Language Immersion Education

U.S. Department of Education, Office of English Language Acquisition, *Dual Language Education Programs: Current State Policies and Practices,*

Washington, D.C. (2015) defines the two main models of dual language programs as:

- Two-way dual language programs (also known as two-way immersion programs), in which ELs who are fluent in the partner language and English-speaking peers are integrated to receive instruction in both English and the partner language.
- One-way dual language programs, in which students from predominantly one language group receive instruction in both English and a partner language. One-way dual language programs may serve predominantly ELs (also known as developmental or maintenance bilingual programs); predominantly English-speaking students (also known as one-way/world language immersion programs); or predominantly students with a family background or cultural connection to the partner language (also known as heritage or native language programs).

For the purpose of the book, I focus on the first model, two-way dual language programs (TWI).

The Center of Applied Linguistics (2011) defined TWI as dual language programs in which both native English speakers and native speakers of the partner language are enrolled, neither group making up more than two thirds of the student population. According to Howard et al. (2003), "TWI is an instructional approach that integrates native English speakers and native speakers of another language and provides instruction to both groups of students in both languages" (p. 1). Programs that aim to reach bilingualism, biliteracy, high academic performance, and cross-cultural competence hold great promise for increasing student achievement, not only for language minority students, but also for native English speakers (Monroy, 2012). TWI schools are designed to build bridges across linguistically heterogeneous student bodies with the goals of bilingualism, academic excellence, and cross-cultural appreciation (Scanlan & Palmer, 2009).

Howard et al. (2003) declared the three defining criteria of a TWI program as follows: (1) fairly equal number of language minority and majority students, (2) minority and majority students are grouped together for core academic instruction, and (3) core academic instructions happen in both languages. These dual language methods increase the opportunity to become bilingual (Alanis & Rodriguez, 2008), as they promise to expand language resources by conserving the language skills that minority students bring with them, and adding another language to the repertoire of English-speaking students *in addition to* offering the hope of improving relationships between language-majority and language-minority groups by enhancing cross-cultural understanding and appreciation (Christian, 1996).

The first dual language program in the United States was established in 1963 at Coral Way Elementary School in Dade County, Florida, serving the children of Cuban immigrants, yet open to English speakers, and providing instructions in Spanish and English to both groups (Monroy, 2012). Members of the Cuban community fleeing the Castro regime believed that their children would return to Cuban schools and, therefore, wanted to teach them Spanish, which soon resulted in another 14 such schools to be set up in Dade County (Potowski, 2007). A parent stated that Coral Way Elementary is an extension of what their families value: an identity rooted in both their Latino culture and their love for this country (Sanchez, 2011). In the 1970s, programs were formed in Washington, D.C.; Chicago, Illinois; and San Diego, California with positive results; however, there was little research published to document their success (Lindholm-Leary, 2001). Of the 422 language immersion programs in the United States (Center for Applied Linguistics, 2011), 312 TWI programs are implemented in California, first established in San Francisco, San Jose, Windsor, Santa Monica, and Oakland during the 1980s (California Department of Education, 2014).

Dual language programs provide literacy and content instruction in English and the partner language for an extended period of time (minimally K-5, preferably K-12) and promote additive bilingualism, which is the process of developing a second language while maintaining the first (Lambert & Tucker, 1972). What defines dual language as immersion education (as opposed to transitional bilingual or foreign language education) is that these programs use the partner language for at least 50% of instruction at all grade levels and teach language through academic content, rather than as a separate subject. Some programs, called 90/10, use the partner language for about 90% of the day in Kindergarten, increasing the amount of English used year by year until each language is used 50% of the time by about third grade. In 90/10 programs, initial literacy instruction is provided in the partner language to all students. In contrast, 50/50 programs use each language 50% of the time from Kindergarten on.

Because native Spanish speakers are the largest group of English language learners in the U.S., the vast majority of dual language programs are Spanish/English, although a handful of programs exist where the partner language is Chinese, French, German, Japanese, or Korean (Center for Applied Linguistics, 2012). Historically, the classic dual language population in Spanish/English programs has been middle-class, European-American native English speakers (NES) and working-class, Latino native Spanish speakers (NSS), although such class and ethnic distinctions are not always clear-cut (Howard & Sugarman, 2001). As the number of dual language programs has grown, they have become increasingly diverse, with some serving 100% Latino populations, some with a significant number of African-Americans, and some serving native speakers of languages other than English or the partner language (Center for Applied Linguistics, 2012). The fact that dual language programs serve historically marginalized, and the fact that they are an intentional meeting point of students from different cultures, ethnicities, language groups, and socioeconomic classes, makes the notion of equity an important focus of program implementation and dual language research.

The Development of Dual Language Programs

The modern era of bilingual education was born out of a recognition of unacceptably poor test scores and long-term outcomes for "English language learners (ELs)"[1] in U.S. schools. The 1968 Bilingual Education Act (enacted as Title VII of the Elementary and Secondary Education Act) was designed to provide federal funds for the education of "ELs" whose academic performance was poor compared to fluent English speakers. The Supreme Court decision in Lau v. Nichols (1974) stated that "ELs" could not receive an education equal to English speakers when they were instructed in a language they did not understand. This decision paved the way for bilingual education as an accommodation for "ELs" (Baker, 2006).

Great controversy ensued (and continues to this day) over how "ELs" should be educated. Throughout these debates, both pro- and anti-bilingual advocates have argued their case on the basis that their approach will lead to greater educational success of "ELs" (and then to economic success and integration into the American way of life), and both sides have used notions of equity to support their case (Cummins, 2000). Pro-bilingual advocates point to decades of research that indicate that using the native language for instruction helps "ELs" develop higher levels of English proficiency (August & Shanahan, 2006; Genesee, Lindholm-Leary, Saunders, & Christian, 2006), while anti-bilingual advocates rely on the logical, albeit scientifically unsupportable assertion that students who need to learn English should spend all of their time in an English-medium environment so as to maximize their access to English and academic content (Cummins, 2000).

I would argue that the debate is nearing its end. In their 2012–2013 Consolidated State Performance Reports (CSPRs), 39 states and the District of Columbia indicated that districts receiving federal Title III funding implemented at least one dual language program that year. In total, these programs featured more than 30 different partner languages. States most frequently reported dual language programs with Spanish (35 states and the District of Columbia), Chinese (14 states), Native American languages (12 states), and French (seven states and the District of Columbia) as the partner languages. State efforts to help recruit and retain students in dual language programs include providing outreach materials and support to inform parents and students about dual language programs (six states); offering a state Seal of Biliteracy to recognize high school graduates who attain proficiency in two languages (11 states and the District of Columbia); and creating opportunities for students to earn university course credit in high school (two states).

Delaware, Georgia, New Mexico, North Carolina, Rhode Island, Utah, and Washington have all developed explicit goals or value statements promoting the use of dual language or bilingual education programs. Among these, Delaware, Georgia, and Utah have established initiatives specifically focused on dual language education. Five states (Connecticut, Illinois, New Jersey, New York, and Texas) mandate that districts provide bilingual education if they have 20 or more "ELs" in the same grade level from the same language background, and schools can implement dual language programs to meet this requirement. Four states have explicit laws constraining the use of bilingual education for "ELs." In Arizona, "ELs" may only participate in a bilingual education program if prior written, informed consent is given annually by the child's parents or legal guardian. Massachusetts's law restricts bilingual education in a similar manner, although an exception exists for two-way dual language and world language programs. New Hampshire state law requires English-only instruction for all students, although bilingual programs are permitted with prior approval from the state board and local school district.

Limitations of Dual Language Programs

For all of its successes, dual language instruction is not without challenges. In the following paragraphs, I focus on the complexities specific to the development or implementation of DLI programs.

Issues of Power and Language

Valdés (1997) provided one of the first studies to critically examine DLI education through the lens of language and power. She makes three important arguments speaking directly to the teachers and administrators of dual language programs, who are acting as policymakers in the arena of language policy for language minority students and low socio-economic Latino families.

Since Spanish is a primary language for the language minority students or a heritage language for the Latino students for whom English may be a primary language, the quality of the Spanish these students receive is of utmost importance. Because the Spanish language may be altered to the modification of English dominant students, it is crucial that teachers ensure that the language minority students receive high quality and linguistically challenging primary language instruction.

DLI programs are also, many times, aimed at bringing in children from outside of the physical community, as language, through the overt goals of the program, serves as a medium for cultural and ethnic understanding and awareness. Valdés (1997) warns that there are social interactions that hold meaning, whether positive or negative, in the larger context of society. DLI programs, with positive intentions, bring together groups of students with ambitions, but not necessarily strategies to teach students how to form meaningful interactions that their society in general may not promote. Although students, teachers, and administrators have positive intention for the program, they may be inviting social interactions into their schools that they are not aware of, or are not skilled in facilitating. Palmer (2010) and Freeman (2000) highlight issues that occur when DLI programs only consider language factors in the inception stages, ignoring things like race, only to face difficulties when power struggles between groups arise as inequalities become apparent.

Language and power are central to Valdés's third point (1997). The vocabulary and language used in the discussions on dual language programs need to be consistent to all ethnic and language groups. Was economic advantage always discussed with Latino parents as with white parents? Were the successes of native Spanish speakers attaining English fluency as recognized as the white child speaking Spanish? Inconsistent language and unspoken messages could not only promote inequality of languages (Palmer, 2010), but could also undermine the intended goals of promoting cultural understanding among groups (Christian, 1996).

There are more and more critical studies on the impact of DLI education. Pimentel et al. (2008) look at the critical issue of who stands to gain the most from dual language programs—or in the framework of power and privilege, which groups make the biggest academic and linguistic gains. It also examines issues of power not only among the participants, but also between the languages. Drawing off Valdés's research (1997), Pimentel et al. pose the idea that the very nature of enrollment strategies of dual language programs in creating linguistic balance (the goal being the balance of native English and Spanish language speakers) also create racial dynamics that are not accounted for in the research, or prepared for in the actual construction of the programs.

Open enrollment laws in Arizona that allow students from the entire metropolitan region to enroll in any school, not limited to the geographic borders of the school or district enrollment area, allow for imbalances in dual language programs. Many times the Spanish speakers are coming to the school from within the areas of the school, whereas many English speakers are coming not only from the immediate school region, but also outlying regions. Research shows that Spanish speakers in the program are often lower socioeconomic students, whereas the English-speaking students vary to a higher degree with many coming from affluent backgrounds. The racial, social, and economic disparities in the program affect student interactions, language usage, perceptions of the purpose of language, as well as parental dynamics that are unaccounted for.

Amrein and Peña (2000) point out some of the challenges of DLI programs within the contextual framework of asymmetry. They view major inequalities such as giving English greater value and status by way of instructional, resource, and student asymmetry, which is clearly not an intentional goal of DLI education. Instructional asymmetry was evident in interviews with an English dual language teacher who claimed that students were learning English faster than when he was an ESL teacher. The statement implied that English acquisition was the goal of the program, rather than equal growth of both English and Spanish. López and Franquíz (2010) noted teachers speaking in dual language classrooms *about* the language (singular) students speak, when the reference should have been plural in an environment promoting bilingualism. Bearse and de Jong (2008) also note that instructional asymmetry can be seen at the secondary level. These students have fewer opportunities to hear and use Spanish, as English content instruction dominates these programs.

Greater asymmetry was noted in regard to resources. English classrooms had far greater print resources than Spanish classrooms. The shelving in the school resource rooms had five times as many resources in English than in Spanish. Spanish classrooms had many posters with English/Spanish translations, whereas in the English classrooms, only English posters were evident, ensuring greater visibility of English print. Beyond this, the further up in grade level students progressed, the less likely they were to find cognitively and linguistically appropriate material.

Although multicultural understanding is commonly cited as a goal of DLI programs, when students in dual language classrooms had opportunities to freely associate in peer groupings, racial imbalance occurred (Amrein & Peña, 2000). This was seen in free class time, on the playground, and in formal groupings for instructional purposes, during which language majority and language minority students would segregate themselves from each other. In situations where the English language model students were predominantly African-American, different issues of what is considered English fluency affected this as well (Palmer, 2010; Scanlan & Palmer, 2009). Research ultimately shows a necessity for balance among language majority and minority students (Amrein & Peña, 2000; Quintanar-Sarellana, 2004).

In addition to racial disparities, select students were called upon to be "language brokers" for students who had difficulty understanding. These students were fully bilingual in both English and Spanish, and would occasionally translate into Spanish for the language minority students and translate into English for the language majority students. However, as Fitts (2006) asserts, not all bilinguals are seen as equally bilingual, and at times those who are bilingual are asked to choose which language is the strongest, in fact denying a student's true sense of bilingualism. In their free time, the language brokers were witnessed either associating together as a separate group (with significant conversation being made in English), or associating with the monolingual English students. In both instances, the language brokers would tend to use English for significant conversations. Fitts also underscores the instances in classrooms when the Spanish language classroom was so controlled that Spanish language usage was strictly monitored, and as a result, was rarely used for natural language. This again highlights the issues of language and power central to the criticisms of dual language programs (Fitts, 2006; Valdés, 1997).

Lastly, Cervantes-Soon (2014) unpacks DLI education against the backdrop of globalization and neoliberal discourses. She sheds much needed light on the commodification of Latinx linguistic resources which perpetuate unequal power relations between majority and minority groups in DLI programs. In her review of the literature, she writes:

By definition, TWI programs must meet diverse needs while working with and integrating communities that differ not only linguistically but also in their social status and resources, parents with conflicting priorities and expectations, educators with varied professional interests and philosophies, and children with different experiences and needs. While English-speaking parents might be committed to social justice, they are also very active in advocating for their children's benefits (Delgado-Larocco, 1998) and may receive a higher degree of attention (Dorner, 2011; Smith, 2001). Equity is also difficult to achieve when the curriculum, acceptable knowledge, and notions of success have already been defined by Eurocentric cultural values (Apple, 1990) and reflected in the languages, experiences, and cultural capital valued by the school and out-side community and by current accountability measures. This context generates issues of power, which play an important role in what happens in the classroom, as well as in the shaping of students' identities and social positions (Potowski, 2007).

In (2017), the authors expand on the working of neoliberal ideology to commodify language skills in DLI programs. In their review of the literature they find:

The critical discourse analysis of five newspapers' framing of TWI in Utah uncovered how a global human capital framework, which focused on commerce and future employment, overshadowed an equity/heritage framework on language maintenance and community (Valdez et al., 2014). Similarly, the Spanish language was commodified in a California school, as native English-speaking parents talked about it as a "useful tool" for their children to communicate with "workers" (Muro, 2016). Opportunity for their children to learn from "live specimens" (Petrovic, 2005, p. 406) while practicing their Spanish was positioned by the dominant group as an added bonus that should be commodified in striving to increase one's human capital. In this process, "white bilingualism is interpreted as an achievement to be acknowledged, and Latino bilingualism one to be anticipated" (Muro, 2016, p. 11). These studies have revealed the reconfiguration of TWI through hegemonic Whiteness. (Flores, 2016)

Neoliberal discourses in education, such as an imperative to prioritize economic markets/exchanges in all interactions (Cervantes-Soon, 2014), have fostered a punitive and largely monolingual accountability system that undermines schools' abilities to meet TWI's bilingual and biliteracy goals. For example, the demands of standardized testing contributed to one TWI program's decision to abandon its biliteracy goals for several months in order to prepare students for tests only in students' stronger language (Palmer, Henderson, Wall, Zúñiga, & Berthelsen, 2015). This decision was especially damaging to language-minoritized students. Despite their bilingualism, they experienced primarily monolingual instruction in English, rather than drawing on their full linguistic repertoire and continuing to develop their bilingualism.

Voices from the Field—Olga Grimalt, Ed.D.
Becoming a Teacher

I became a bilingual teacher in a non-conventional way. I spent a number of years wandering the job circuit in my 20's, enrolling in a Master's degree in writing with a deep desire to find a purpose in the day-to-day reality of needing to be employed. There were many who encouraged me to become a teacher however I scoffed at the idea thinking, "Me, plus a room full of children? No way." But in the summer of 1990, with a need to find a job that would offer me health insurance and the prospect of having summers off to write, I walked into the doors of the Los Angeles Unified School District (LAUSD) and asked, "Are you hiring emergency credentialed teachers?" I was told no. Accepting that answer, I left but once I reached my car it occurred to me that perhaps I should've told the receptionist, I'm bilingual. I went back, offered what I thought was a small detail and found myself being hired on the spot. What I didn't know that day, as I signed my first contract, was that I was about to fall in love.

The first day of my career as an elementary bilingual teacher, I knew very little about teaching; what I did know was the joy I felt upon seeing the faces of the eight and nine year olds who looked at me with the anticipation of a new school year, unaware that I was new, 'green new.' I was excited at the prospect of teaching in my two languages, Spanish and English, but from that first day I learned that teaching was not the only role I would take; becoming an advocate for the students and families who trusted me unconditionally, drove my passion to teach. It was clear to me that my students, who were being bussed from downtown Los Angeles to the west San Fernando Valley, riding a bus one hour each way, had no voice on our campus, in fact a vast majority of the school community resented that the district had established a bilingual program; essentially the bilingual students were not welcomed there.

I spent the school year learning how to teach my students reading, math, social studies and science but I also found myself talking to them about the importance of being bilingual, and how their first language was an asset in our classroom. In those days, the prevalent model of bilingual education was a transitional model, where primary language instruction was used as a vehicle to accessing English. The focus was to develop academics through the child's mother tongue, as they learned and became proficient in English. It wasn't about becoming bilingual, it was about becoming English proficient. That was the bilingual program I had been assigned to, however for me it was always about being bilingual and honoring the language the students brought to the classroom. I knew by the end of my first month, that teaching had found me and not for the sole purpose of teaching reading, writing, math, social studies and science to third graders but for the added purpose of becoming a supporter and promoter of bilingual education.

The Glory Years

I'm fortunate that I came into teaching when I did, pre-NCLB, when standardized testing existed but wasn't glorified. The atmosphere was inviting, engaging and forgiving for new teachers. This was 1990 California, when bilingual education was widespread across the state and the need for bilingual teachers increased each school year. After beginning my career in LAUSD, I moved to Long Beach and joined the Long Beach Unified School District (LBUSD) where

I would spend most of my classroom years. I again joined a district that was in the midst of establishing bilingual programs. In Long Beach, our programs served both Spanish and Khmer speaking children and again, the prevalent model was a transitional model that developed a child's primary language typically through third grade. The goal was to transition the students to all English instruction.

As bilingual teachers in the district, we advocated for parents' rights to select the bilingual program strand at their schools, we pushed for adequate supplemental materials in the non-English languages and we continued to promote bilingualism informally. As in my previous district, the goal of the bilingual program was the attainment of English and although I knew that after the students left my third-grade classroom and moved on to fourth grade, their instruction would be mostly in English I still wanted them to maintain their Spanish. I recall one afternoon as I crossed the playground, one of my former third grade students, now a fifth grader, approaching me to say hello. She initiated the conversation in English, I responded in Spanish, she answered in English. I said to her, "Why are you speaking to me in English?" She looked at me perplexed by the question. "Don't forget that Spanish is important too." She smiled and ran off. As I watched her join her friends, all Spanish speakers, I knew they were speaking mostly if not exclusively in English. It made me sad. At the time, I was beginning to truly understand the status of English and the subtle but powerful messages the students were receiving that English was more important. My monologues in class about the importance of being bilingual and preserving their first language was being overrun by the dominant language: English. I call these initial years of teaching the "Glory Years" because I was left alone, unrestricted by state and federal mandates, and although bilingual education was riding a positive wave, as a bilingual educator I was always working against the current. Lurking around the corner of those "Glory Years" was an anti-immigrant, anti-bilingual education sentiment that rippled through California. Bilingual education as we all knew it was about to crumble.

The Wall Came Falling Down

In 1994, early in my teaching career, Proposition 187 was passed by California voters. The ballot initiative sought to prohibit non-documented residents of California from using health care facilities, public education and other social services. When Proposition 187 passed, I found myself not only advocating for the rights of Latino students in bilingual programs, but also fighting for the right of those same students to simply be allowed to attend school. California's constitution establishes a fundamental right to a free education for all students, however Proposition 187 now required school personnel to screen students and deny an education to those who were not residents or citizens. Ultimately the law was challenged in the court and never enacted, but it instilled a fear among students and parents.

Then came Proposition 227. This initiative targeted students who were English learners enrolled in a bilingual program. A group of bilingual educators and I spent countless hours in the 1997–1998 school year organizing fundraisers and walking precincts. We set up "No on Proposition 227" tables at various events with the intent of talking to California voters about the ideological venom of Proposition 227. Sure, "English for the Children" was the message on the surface of this initiative, but we all knew that the resentment against immigrant children invading our public schools and being instructed in a language other than English was the impetus behind this initiative. I spoke to many people who would claim, "This is America." "Students should learn English." It didn't matter if I explained that in a bilingual program the students do learn English. It didn't matter if I explained that other countries taught children a second language from the moment they entered school. Most people I spoke to believed that bilingual education meant that students were being instructed exclusively in Spanish. The idea that anyone would think that I would want the students in my classroom to only learn Spanish was ludicrous; but the anti-immigrant atmosphere that was pervasive across the state convinced voters that bilingual education was wrong.

The most dedicated bilingual teachers worked tirelessly to defeat the proposition. In my district, a group of bilingual educators including myself organized 500 plus teachers, parents and other community supporters to descend on the LBUSD board meeting on two occasions. We were adamant that the district take a stand against the proposition and defend the numerous students who were receiving primary language instruction. Disappointedly, LBUSD's board of education remained neutral; they never took a stand for or against the proposition. It was clear the district had no intention of supporting primary language instruction, in fact it felt more like district administrators and the board of education were eager to let it go.

Dismantling Bilingual Programs

During the implementation year of Proposition 227, I was a teacher on special assignment in the district's Program Assistance for Language Minority Students office. I spent the better part of the school year alongside the literacy coaches providing professional development for teachers in our elementary schools. The political climate was intense as I watched the district strip students of an educational program due to the whim of California voters. It was disheartening to know that the general public including people who are not educators felt empowered to make an educational decision for a population of students who held no power whatsoever in their fate as students within our public school system. As a bilingual person, it angered me that by simply filling in the "yes" box on a ballot, a decision was made that affected 25% of English learners in our state. A few months after the proposition passed, district warehouse trucks arrived at schools with bilingual programs to pick up all the non-English books. One day I went to our district warehouse and found hundreds of Spanish and Khmer books thrown into a huge pile in the middle of the warehouse. A huge mound of books, surrounded by desks, chairs, and bookshelves, waiting to be discarded because every one of those books was replaced by an English equivalent. At that moment, I knew it was time to go back to the classroom. By the end of that school year, I left my position in the district office and once again became a third-grade bilingual teacher but this time in a two-way immersion program.

Two-Way Bilingual Immersion Programs

I returned to the classroom as a bilingual teacher on the heels of Proposition 227. Although the district had gotten rid of the majority of the bilingual programs across the city, it "saved" the Two-Way Bilingual Immersion program being implemented at a handful of sites. Yes, this program was spared the ax of Prop. 227, but the atmosphere was heavy. No one trusted the district or the board of education, and our team of bilingual teachers were always on edge, waiting anxiously for the board of education to change their minds and pull the rug out from under us. We became very protective of the program and were ready to fight if we sensed that the district may close us down.

In the midst of anxiety surrounding this time, I was excited to return to the classroom and continue the work of teaching students in two languages. This program was different, along with teaching Latino Spanish speakers, I was also teaching students who were learning Spanish as a second language. Students who were fluent Spanish speakers were learning alongside students who were fluent English speakers. The goal of this program was bilingualism and biliteracy. After struggling with my former students to value their ability to speak, read and write Spanish, I now found myself in a program in which the goal was for all students to become bilingual and biliterate. Once again, fell in love with teaching. It was the experience at the two-way school that solidified my passion and commitment to the idea that all students should have the opportunity to learn two languages from the moment they enter kindergarten. As always, I embraced the opportunity to teach in two languages and impressed on the students continuously the importance of becoming fluent in two languages. I loved having both Spanish dominant/English learners and English dominant/

Spanish learners in the same classroom. I embraced the possibilities of creating a classroom environment where students of different backgrounds, different ethnicities can learn together in not only one language but two. I found myself feeling a deep sense of passion at providing a space where language development was embraced, this time in a program that allowed the fluent Spanish speakers to continue to develop their primary language.

I worked with a team of bilingual teachers who were dedicated to the development of bilingualism and who were also protective of the two-way program and willing to do what was needed to ensure that the district didn't shut us down. Once I again I found myself in a situation where being a bilingual teacher was only one role. The role of advocate became prominent again in protecting the program but for me it also became evident that the English monolingual families carried a certain amount of power that the Latino families did not. And so there I was again providing a voice for the Latino families enrolled in the program in the midst of looking for ways to positively promote our program and the idea of bilingualism.

Our team began to look for ways to showcase our program. It was clear the district would allow us to exist but no one in a position of power was going to advocate for the program. Our team took on that role. We looked for ways to empower our parents and advocate for the bilingual development of all the students in the program. We decided to present our program to those who ultimately had the power to allow us to continue to do the work we loved. We prepared a presentation for our board of education. We selected two students to address the board: one had started the program as English-only, the other had started the program as a fluent Spanish speaker learning English as a second language. Each student spoke of the benefits of becoming bilingual. Although the intent of the presentation was to showcase how this program includes both English and Spanish speakers, I was shocked to find that when the English only student finished speaking in Spanish, the audience erupted in applause but when the Latino student addressed the board in English, she only received a lukewarm applause. I realized at that moment that learning Spanish as a second language was held to higher esteem than learning English as a second language. For me this was a wake-up call and I once again found myself advocating for those who didn't have a strong voice. I was disheartened to discover that even in a two-way immersion program, Spanish could still occupy a 'less-than' status and I found myself, once again, defending the program and taking on the role of advocate for the Latino English learner students.

Changing of the Guard
The atmosphere, since the late 90s, surrounding bilingual education in California has been negative and dim however the last few years a shift is

occurring. Two-way immersion programs are becoming more common across the state, allowing both Spanish and English speakers to benefit from bilingual development. Communities are beginning to demand that their schools implement a two-way program so that their children can benefit from learning a new language at a young age.

In November 2016, California voters passed Proposition 58, overturning the restrictive policies under Proposition 227. The obstacles of implementing a bilingual program have been removed and now two-way immersion programs are growing rapidly across the state and the country. The difference pre-Proposition 227 and post-Proposition 58? Two-way immersion programs include both majority speaking students and minority speaking students. Pre-Proposition 227, most bilingual programs were for non-English speaking students, now most programs bring together both the non-English speaking or bilingual student with the English-only speaker and together they learn the two languages; they learn each other's language. The caution here however is being careful of the subtle ways that the English speaker is glorified for learning a new language, and how the English-learner is expected to learn English fluently. Both the Spanish speaker and monolingual English speaker in the program are developing bilingual skills, both bring their first language to the classroom, but the acquisition of English for the English learner is viewed as "not a big deal" because English still holds more power. The perspective from the outside hasn't changed. The English learner is expected to learn English, and the fact that they are bilingual is inconsequential, however the monolingual English speaker, who is learning Spanish as a second language is viewed as accomplishing something above and beyond, even though both groups of students are becoming bilingual/biliterate side by side. Two-way immersion programs hold the most promise for the development of bilingualism, but we still need to be on guard to ensure that our bilingual students, those entering the classroom with a language other than English, have a prominent place at the classroom table. We still struggle to ensure that their first language is valued as much as English. Although we are now in an era that embraces the development of bilingualism, there is still work to be done.

Fall 2017 marks the beginning of my 28th year as a bilingual educator. I now dedicate my time working as a dual language consultant, supporting schools across the state and the country in the implementation of two-way immersion programs. It is my hope that bilingual educators will embrace the current positive climate to ensure that high quality bilingual programs are implemented and most importantly that the programs are open for all students. The prize is biliteracy: to develop two languages fully through all domains of language across content areas. We have a responsibility to ensure that all students have access and that English learners in particular have the opportunity to develop and *maintain* their first language while becoming proficient in English. Their development of bilingualism is equally important. We must move forward with the belief that each child enrolled in a two-way immersion program has the ability and the right to be bilingual/biliterate.

Many years have passed since I walked into my first bilingual classroom, but the dedication and passion of teaching in two languages has not waned. I now find myself in a moment where multilingualism is being embraced but I also know how quickly the tide can change. While we are once again riding a positive wave in bilingual education, our commitment must be unwavering. The time for our students to shine is now and it is with two-way immersion that we hold the promise that each and every child has the right to become bilingual and biliterate in our 21st century global society.

Implementing DLI Programs: A Mixed Bag

A qualitative study was conducted in New York City to learn more about the relationship between DLI program labels and the implementation of these programs in public schools. Researchers found that many self-designated DLI schools did not actually possess the basic qualities descriptive of a DLI program (Torres-Guzmán, Kleyn, Morales-Rodríguez, & Han, 2005). The study was carried out using qualitative data from surveys created by one of the researchers in collaboration with New York City public schools, which had an 85% return rate from the sixty schools they were distributed to.

Teachers at these DLI schools answered questions about their programs, and the researchers found that many teachers do not understand the basic tenets of DLI programs. The researchers emphasized that these teachers are "participating in decisions or allowing decisions to be made in ignorance of what they ought to be doing" (Torres-Guzmán et al., 2005). This study underscores that the implementation of successful DLI programs relies heavily on the knowledge their teachers, and their understanding of the model. A solid foundational understanding of the DLI models in place needs to be possessed by the teachers in order to establish and sustain programs that are truly DLI programs (Torres-Guzmán et al., 2005). If teachers do not have a clear understanding of the foundation of the DLI program, it creates a major obstacle in establishing and sustaining a successful DLI program.

Two other critical obstacles that are closely connected to each other are: (1) rushing the implementation of new DLI programs, and (2) the lack of foundational training for DLI teachers. Although starting a new DLI program can be an exciting opportunity, pressures to get the program started quickly may hinder the program from having a comprehensive master plan by the time the first students enter the classroom. Excited parents, administrators, and community members may push for programs to open as soon as possible, without consideration for the necessary, thorough planning that a DLI program requires (Montague, 1997). The risk of implementing a new DLI program too quickly is that it may be implemented poorly, and its lack of success could contribute to pervasive stigmas around bilingual education programs (Gomez et al., 2005).

Aside from harming its reputation with local communities, a DLI program that is implemented too quickly (and as a result, poorly) may also harm the relations and understandings of the program at the school level. This is illustrated by the lack of information and understanding that teachers have in regard to how a DLI program functions, and of what it offers to students, so as to accurately qualify as a true DLI program (Torres-Guzman, 2005). Without teachers having shared understandings of their program, the foundation and integrity of the DLI program is questioned.

Furthermore, a growing number of programs around the country, paired with a scarcity of teachers with the necessary language skills, have led to a shortage of qualified dual language teachers. A report issued by the U.S. Department of Education's Office of Postsecondary Education (2015) indicates that 16 states identified bilingual education as a teacher shortage area for the 2015–2016 school year. States have pursued a variety of strategies to expand the supply of dual language teachers, including creating alternative certification pathways, establishing partnerships with other countries to identify teachers with appropriate partner language skills, increasing recruitment efforts, forming partnerships with teacher preparation programs, and providing financial incentives for teachers.

DLI Research

Much of the research and meta-analyses of evidence for and against alternative models of language-in-education have focused on programs in the United States (e.g., Krashen, 1996, 1999; Lee, 1996; Rossell & Baker, 1996), where English is the overwhelmingly dominant language in education, trade, law, and government. The United States has strongly assimilationist language and education policies, a comparatively rich resource base, and relatively high levels of teacher training. That said, the generalizability of findings from American studies must be questioned.

Attempts at controlled empirical studies are riddled with methodological shortcomings and inconsistencies across disciplines. For example, in a review of seven major evaluations of bilingual programs, Cziko (1992) notes that this body of research cannot be used to draw any conclusions about whether bilingual education is necessary or successful. Of the seven studies Cziko reviews, only one includes research from outside of the United States. He cites several issues with the evaluations of bilingual research programs:

a. lack of adequate random-sampling procedures, resulting in questionable generalizations of findings;
b. lack of control of confounding factors in assessing treatment effects;
c. questionable reliability and validity of achievement measures, particularly when used for minority language students;
d. bias in the selection of studies for review; and
e. inappropriate use of statistical procedures in analyzing evaluation findings and synthesizing the results of many studies (as in meta-analysis).

These issues, among others, reinforce the need to be critical of findings in studies conducted on dual language programs in the United States, as well as the need to dig deeper into the research that has already be done, so as to uncover other possible interpretations of the data, and inform future studies and methodologies.

Where Are We Now?

Most of the authors cited above, who provide more critical analyses of DLI programs conclude with a return to DLI as a potential site for equity and justice. Cervantes-Soon (2014) concludes:

> The potential of these TWI programs to set a new directions in the education of Latin@ children is not small. Thus, I hope that by shedding light on the intricacies of newly Latinized contexts in which TWI programs operate, educators, policy makers, and program planners can gain some insight into the tremendous project of human agency in which Latin@ families engage every day and use it to inform the development and implementation of more-empowering dual-language programs and to humanize the learning experiences of all children.

As Cervantes-Soon and Palmer et point out, there are much larger issue at play, specifically the ideologies of neoliberalism and global capitalism.

Thus, how DLI programs disentangle themselves from the insidious forces of neoliberalism emerges as one of the most significant challenges DLI schools will need to address.

In the following paragraphs, I will connect how neoliberal forces, particularly via assessment and accountability, dehumanize schools. It is imperative that we identify these connections if we are committed to DLI schools as sites that sustain and revitalize our children's humanity. *Our educational institutions are dangerous to children, and in many ways to our teachers. Stripping away autonomy, creativity, and intellectualism from our classrooms affronts the humanness that is central to a dynamic and vibrant education.*

No one can argue that human capital theory is what has ultimately gained currency in education. The subject areas that receive the greatest resources are those associated with earning a living. This means that a valuable education is that which increases students' contribution in the market economy. As stated previously by several scholars, a bilingual students' contribution in the global economic market is often used as an argument for the benefits of bilingual schools.

According to human capital theory, the primary purpose of education is to produce as many productive workers as possible in a competitive labor force. Conversely, Kohn (1986) asserts, "Superior performance not only does not require competition; it usually seems to require its absence" (pp. 46–47). Through competition, students are unable to define themselves and discover their unique, personal means to happiness. Without rigorous, performance-based competition, students would be able to breathe and work at their own pace, ultimately elevating their level of performance. The scarcity of "A's" pushes students to repress their natural abilities, ultimately stifling their sense of self-worth.

In recent years, the "accountability" movement in education's increased interest in efficiency—that is, its increased interest in setting measurable ends, and then working to achieve those ends as efficiently as possible—has manifest itself (perhaps most acutely) in standardized testing. K-12 students often find themselves defined by their standardized tests scores, as their ability to pursue higher education, follow their dreams, or make the "first cut" when applying to schools depends heavily on their standardized test scores. These tests are viewed as reliable cognitive benchmarks of performance that should be administered regularly.

That being said, there is little or no evidence of concern regarding the negative effects of frequent standardized testing on curriculum. For example, teachers teaching "to the test," putting nothing into lesson plans except what will later require recall for their students' standardized tests. This type of teaching is detrimental, as students are left with monotonous lessons and test-based knowledge. In addition, there is even less evidence of concern about the discouraging impasse that students face when they experience repeated failure—not ready or able to learn how to "master" these tests. If students cannot conquer standardized tests, they feel helpless, worthless, and self-defeated.

Sadly, more empathetic modes of knowledge have been sacrificed as performance variables because they are too difficult to measure. These forms of knowledge include: affective knowledge (including self esteem and caring about others), emotional intelligence (including anger management and interpersonal communication), the love of learning, the ability to express oneself in front of a group, the ability to relate to one's peers, the ability to work cooperatively, and the ability to exercise creativity in problem solving. As a result of the aforementioned emphasis on cognitive efficiency and learning what can be easily measured, there is very little in secondary school curriculum that is geared toward simply having fun with learning, or appreciating learning for its own sake.

In a world where output is measured by performance on standardized tests, learning is seen as most efficient when teachers concentrate on cognitive learning and disregard other learning outcomes. Standardized testing suggests that it does not matter how students *feel* about what they learn, or indeed how they feel about learning in general. What is important is that they are able to answer cognitive questions correctly on tests. This defeats one of the major purposes of education: the foundation of a love of learning.

Standardized testing is historically and politically linked to a business model for operating schools since the early 20th century (Darder & Torres, 2004). Corporate leaders have maintained this control for over a century, largely due to the close alignment of standardized test scores to district accountability. Darder and Torres (2005) assert that businessmen are closely aligned to the idea that schools should now function with the efficiency of a for-profit business. They insist that measurable, scientifically based objectives should be the primary impetus for making decisions, designing curricula, and articulating pedagogical imperatives of the classroom (p. 209).

Because economic stimulation from the new education standards, Common Core State Standards (CCSS), generated revenue into the pockets of big-name education corporations, the United States has neglected investing in their teachers or within local schools. This financially irresponsible reaction to CCSS is due to the standardized mentality of education. For example, the Los Angeles Unified School District (LAUSD) is the second largest district in the United States, serving over 660,000 students. It recently updated its reading program from its previous Macmillan and McGraw Hill reading series to the Common Core version of Treasures, including a pacing and assessment guide (LAUSD, 2013). And why? Because these reading programs assure districts that their test scores will rise. Kirylo et al. (2010) rightly suggest that this shift in education not only "diverts astronomical amounts of money away from addressing the needs of their children" (p. 333), but also reinforces poor literacy skills, and furthers the achievement gap in oppressed groups because students are not given the time or resources they need to understand and digest

the material. Yet the focus on raising test scores has remained the leading factor in leadership and budgetary decisions on pedagogy (Darder & Torres, 2005;
Giroux, 2004, 2011; Kirylo et al., 2010).

When schools have a strong focus on numbers, measurement, and quanti-
fication, the beliefs and practices (pedagogy) of the teacher shift to instilling
skill sets that favor test taking, leading to practices that "foster memorization
and conformity; promote reductionistic, decontextualized, and fragmented
curriculum; [and] advance mechanistic approaches that are decontextualized
from students' needs" (Salazar, 2013, p. 124). With 45 states, four territories,
the District of Columbia, and the Department of Defense Education Activity
all adopting the CCSS, billions of dollars have traded hands in a surge of new
materials from educational vendors around the world. These materials and
programs are often created with learning objectives, teaching prompts, and a
scripted pacing guide. Rodriguez and Smith (2011) refer to this kind of pedagogy as a one that effectively distances educators from the culture, values, and
voice that give students their humanity.

Unfortunately, DLI schools are not exempt from these pressures. During
interviews conducted at DLI schools in Southern California, several teachers
and parents were concerned that assessment and accountability were elimi-
nating the very thing that drew them to bilingual education in the first place.
To remedy this, teachers were encouraged to tap into the arts, especially music
and drama, to encourage oral language development. At one DLI school, a
teacher spoke about the like-mindedness among the community in regard to
testing, which was basically, "assess the child to inform your teaching":

> I'm not saying testing is bad, but I am saying that too much of it is. Testing
> and its frequency should be seen differently for our bilingual program.
> Language development is not a standard process, so to give kids tests
> every year in English is crazy. But what really angers me is that no one
> uses the data from the test scores—they provide nothing to inform our
> teaching. So then what really is the purpose of this?

During one observation, I watched a 1st grade team spend countless hours
after school translating Common Core standards. Nothing was available in
Spanish. Moreover, in a focus group of Spanish-speaking mothers and two DLI
retired educators, they stressed that when DLI was "unpopular" or perceived
as the renegade child of liberal Latinx and liberal White parents, the district
paid very little attention to the school. There was a "ton of autonomy and
freedom." The progressive ideological base of the parents has shifted. One
parent expanded:

We don't have the hippy white parent who is totally against testing any more. We have a new demographic of white parents who care about the how the school ranks, how their child ranks, etc. They wield a lot of power that isn't overt. It's subtle, but you can feel the shift by the questions that are asked at Open House or during a PTA meeting.

It is clear that as DLI schools grow in number and become more popular for middle class families, accountability and assessment will weigh heavily.

In 2011, the American Council on the Teaching of Foreign Languages (ACTFL) found through a survey of state officials and reviews of SEA websites that 42 states had adopted world language proficiency standards (Phillips & Abbott, 2011). Of the 14 states and the District of Columbia that provided information about their world language proficiency standards on their websites in spring 2015, three states (North Carolina, Ohio, and Utah) have used the ACTFL proficiency scales to set grade-level or grade-span language proficiency targets specific to K–12 dual language programs. Illinois uses Spanish language development standards developed by WIDA to guide Spanish language instruction and assessment for dual language and other bilingual education programs.

Among the 16 states with information about partner language proficiency assessment policies on their SEA website, five states (Delaware, Kentucky, New Mexico, Oregon, and Utah) require state-funded dual language programs to assess students' progress toward developing partner language proficiency at least annually. The remaining 11 states with such information on their websites do not require districts or dual language programs to implement a particular assessment, but they do recommend or provide access to partner language assessment tools. Moreover, case study research on the use of dual language programs also indicates that Title I and Title III requirements that schools demonstrate that "ELs" make adequate progress and meet the same content standards required of native English speaking students have caused some communities to rethink the implementation of dual language programs, and consider implementing an English Only approach (Wright & Choi, 2006; Gandara & Rumberger, 2009; Warhol & Mayer, 2012; Lindholm-Leary, 2012; Menken & Solorza, 2012).

Recent research into four model TWI programs and schools (Howard & Sugarman, 2007) revealed that several qualities characterize the most effective TWI programs. These programs promote bilingualism through developing a culture of intellectualism, which includes a "commitment to ongoing learning," to "collaboration and the exchange of ideas," to the "fostering of independence," and to the "promotion of higher order thinking" (pp. 82–83). They also encourage a culture of equity that values and protects time spent in the minority language, includes students with special needs, addresses the needs of English-dominant and minority language-dominant students in a balanced way, and fosters an appreciation of the multiple cultures represented in the classroom. Finally, these successful schools develop a culture of leadership, challenging teachers, administrators and students alike to take initiative in their own learning, make public presentations, respond to the needs of others, and build consensus and share leadership.

No one would debate these qualities. But they are written without an acknowledgement to the current context of high stakes testing, teacher accountability, the privatization of education, and other oppressive assaults on public education and the education of our linguistic minorities. We need arguments that are more aggressive, more unapologetic, and more honest about what "intercultural understanding" truly implies. If we start with an ideological stance that our children have a human right to multilingual education, then the discourse is elevated to loftier objectives than "high test scores." Objectives that informed the initial movement to DLI, but are now in danger.

Voices from the Field—Shelley Spiegel-Coleman

I had the privilege of interviewing Shelly Spiegel-Coleman[2] at the beginning stages of the study. I was fascinated by her story, a behind the scenes account of her advocacy efforts—on the ground—to implement a DLI program for all children. We often do not hear these stories, which are critical reminders of the original intentions of the DLI community—intentions centered around biliteracy, human dignity, and connection. For Shelly, providing a bilingual education for linguistic minority students in a context that integrated language identities and resources, was a formula to safeguard social equity.

In Her Own Words

My whole career was about this issue. For twenty-seven years, I worked with the LA County Office of Education. I knew at the time that Long Beach Unified did not have a positive or forward-thinking agenda in terms of bilingualism. They had a large population of English learners who were not being afforded the opportunity to become bilingual, to sustain the language of their home and of their parents and of their grandparents. They were losing the language.

I was pregnant when I worked with the LA County Office of Education, so I had a dual motivation: one for the children who needed to sustain their heritage language and the other for my own children. We started to reach out to like-minded people, like the Padillas. We to started meet in our living room to strategize how can we get a bilingual program in Long Beach. So we put up announcements that if anybody would be interested in thinking about a bilingual experience for their children in elementary school, to call us. Word got around that there was a family who lived in Culver City, which did have an immersion program, but they wanted to move to Long Beach. And so they said, if we could guarantee there would be an immersion program in Long Beach, they would move. I told her I couldn't guarantee anything. We're just meeting in my living room trying to get it started ... but then the families started to come.

I was hoping that with 6–7 families, we could influence the District. At the time, there was a bilingual program at Patrick Henry, but it was a short-term K-3 program. We met with the assistant Superintendent, and he actually positive. He basically said well, if you do all the work, and you get all the kids, find the school and a principle, basically do everything, then we will definitely think about supporting it. That's all I needed to hear.

I knew the person in charge of the English Learner program in the District, and I called her and said, which schools do you think would be most receptive? She contacted a few principals who weren't even interested in meeting with us. Finally, one principal at Cubberley was interested, but he insisted we meet the parents to gauge interest. Oh my God, it was horrible. They said terrible things, absolutely terrible things. "Why would we want our children to go to school with those kids?" They literally said that.

So then we met with the principal, Jan McNab, who had the K-3 bilingual transitional program at Patrick Henry. She was very excited, but was concerned about recruiting enough kids. So, we made flyers to recruit Kindergartners and 1st graders for a new bilingual program. At the time, they were bussing kids in from the West side, kids who were Spanish-speaking, and whose parents were supportive about wanting their kids in the program. The kids we needed were the English-speaking kids, right? Everybody passed out flyers wherever they went! One person found a flyer in a rented a condo in Mammoth!

Sure enough, we recruited enough Spanish-speaking and English-speaking kids to start the program. That's how it started. The teachers unfortunately were assigned by the district, we didn't get a say on that, and they were not the best. So we became more aggressive. We formed our own parent group supported by Jan McNab, and we met every month to talk about the program: what could we do to help the teachers, what can we do to help get materials— the materials were an issue, a big issue.

I ended up submitting federal grants through my work at the LA County of Education. With federal funding, we were able to add programs, hire full-time resource teachers to work with the parents and teaches. We also had more influence in terms of hiring, and we were able to recruit really good bilingual teachers.

I really want to mention our two principals, Fred Navarro and Jan McNab. They were wonderful principals. They fought for us. Any time we had problems with the district, Jan would tell us she would go talk to the district, and when she would come back and say, I've done the best I can, it meant now we could do whatever we needed to do. She did not block us putting pressure on the district at all. The parent group really did take the lead on many of the issue. One issue was the bussing, because we were worried that the bussing was going to stop. We sustained the bussing for a few more years. They reduced the number of stops, I remember, but we were able to sustain the bussing. It didn't take long for the reputation of the program to grow. Sometimes I'm just really overwhelmed, when I see the program now, to know where it came from and to where it is now.

I want to make sure that our programs are about bringing both communities together. It feels like now programs are filled with middle-class and upper middle-class families. That was not the intent of this program. The district or the school needs to make that a priority, and save the spaces for Spanish-speakers, address transportation issues, et cetera. Our excellent DLI programs must be available to both sides of our community. The numbers are very small from the Spanish-speaking community and even though we talk about academic results, there are deeper reasons why a Jewish lady like me wanted her kids to attend a bilingual school. I wanted a school that brought together different points of view, a community with a vision for a better world.

Shelly's impressive narrative illuminates the pivotal role of social activism ensure diversity, equity, and human connection in our DLI schools. For Shelly Spiegel-Coleman, the right to languages is fundamentally connected to education for democracy, global citizenry, and social consciousness. For her, the small yet mighty DLI program was the platform to create change for social good.

Conclusion

Despite the fact that the number of students classified as "ELs" has grown and continues to grow, and that DLI programs have in fact made strides, the legacy of No Child Left Behind and English Only policies in education have pushed researchers in the field of bilingual education to focus their attention on the effectiveness of bilingual education, and have pushed those constructing bilingual education programs to build schools on shaky foundations and fail to provide their teachers with adequate training—compromising the success of dual language programs before they even begin. In addition to this, the asymmetry we find in dual language program instruction, resources, and students (problematically favoring English over the partner language) makes it difficult to adequately collect data, as issues of power and language permeate the establishment and execution of these programs.

In the United States, moreover, efficiency and effectiveness have troublingly taken precedence over quality and care in education policy and implementation, leaving us with pedagogical models that fail to view learning and students as ends in and of themselves. To view students as sources of capital—that is, as a *means* to measurable ends—is to dehumanize education, favoring quantity and production over quality and human dignity, and ultimately distancing educators from the humanity of their students.

In light of neoliberal and global capital forces, it will be difficult for DLI programs and schools to protect and deepen a commitment to linguistic human rights. In the next part of the book, I focus on the humanizing work of DLI communities that survive in various pockets. Focusing on bilingual youth and teachers lead me to a new DLI framework committed to the protection of linguistic human rights for our bi/multilingual youth.

Notes

1   I prefer using terms that highlight either people's strengths/diversity or the power structures that frame their lives. For example, when writing about children in TWI programs, I rely on Garcia's work that makes the case for using emergent bilinguals rather than "English Learners;" this term indicates that they engage language(s) other than, or in addition to, English at home.

2   Executive Director of Californians Together, a coalition of 24 statewide professional, parent and civil rights organizations focused on fostering full participation in a democratic society through quality education for children and parents from underserved communities.

PART 2

A Humanizing Dual Language Immersion Education

∴

CHAPTER 4

Intentionality

I lost my talk
The talk you took away.
When I was a little girl
At Shubenacadie school.

You snatched it away:
I speak like you
I think like you
I create like you
The scrambled ballad, about my world.

Two ways I talk
Both ways I say,
Your way is more powerful.

So gently I offer my hand and ask,
Let me find my talk
So I can teach you about me.

RITA JOE

∴

When we consider co-constructing bilingual education with our youth, it is critical we begin with *intention*. Intention refers to the thoughts, beliefs, desires, and hopes of a bilingual program. In essence, it is the starting point of every dream.

Intentions are different than goals in that goals involve envisioning a future outcome in the world, planning how to get there, applying discipline, and working hard to achieve it. Outcomes dictate the vast majority of education programs. When educational constituents organize their time and energy based on outcomes, the future is always the focus: Will the school reach its goal? Will the members of the school community be happy when they do? What's next?

Setting an intention is entirely different than establishing outcomes. The future does not guide an intention—the present does. Being grounded in

© KONINKLIJKE BRILL NV, LEIDEN, 2019 | DOI:10.1163/9789004389724_004

intention is what delivers integrity to a program. Through the skillful cultivation of intention, members of the school community learn to make wise goals and then to work hard toward achieving them without getting caught up in the outcome. This stands in stark contrast to a school community that narrowly focuses on measurable results.

DLI programs that detach from predetermined outcomes live in the wisdom of uncertainty, that is, in the unquestioning belief in the power of children. It perhaps goes without saying that grounding DLI programs in intention is the way in which bilingual education can establish strong foundations, remedying the problems that can flow from program establishment moving too quickly (in hopes of achieving identifiable ends).

Mission statements are evident at most school sites; nonetheless, they primarily outline measurable goals and student outcomes. As DLI programs continue to grow and expand, intentions provide a deeper and richer point of entry to articulate a school community's philosophical stance vis-à-vis the query—What is the purpose of a DLI school? The following are examples of possible intentions:

— We honor the dignity of bilingual children.
— We promote, validate, and utilize the wisdom that bilingual children bring with them.
— We teach and learn our connection to everything: humans, animals, the earth, and the stars.
— We safeguard the education of linguistic minoritized youth.

Intention impels a school community to think more deeply about the purpose of education. Schools often reflect a narrow image of human possibilities and impose restrictive limits on each child's unique potential. Instead of merely preparing children to become "well educated" national citizens, or productive participants in the economic system, a DLI community can express its commitment to inspiring children's creativity, imagination, compassion, social skills, self-knowledge, and emotional health. This type of education cultivates the whole bilingual child, helping youth to live more consciously within their communities and natural ecosystems and to embrace their unique sense of self.

In the following paragraphs, I flesh out possible intentions.

We Promote, Validate, and Utilize the Wisdom That Bilingual Children Bring with Them

Educational policies and practices systematically dismiss the phenomenology of children. Throughout school, educators presume to know what is best for children. In fact, educators' insights just cannot compare to the power of awareness and discernment that already exists within children. From birth, they inherit wisdom that cannot be learned or unlearned—an inherent wisdom that is unique to each. It is vital that we value and honor this incredible element of the self.

Language minoritized youth carry the wisdom of their mother tongue—traditions, norms, and knowledge—within them. For these youth, being schooled in the United States comes at a cost in that they are forced to leave their language, their ways of knowing and being. Recent scholarship by Paris and Alim (2014) underscore the fallacy of measuring youth in our communities solely against the White middle-class norms of knowing and being that continue to dominate notions of educational achievement. They write:

Du Bois (1965) of course, theorized this over a century ago with his conceptualization of double consciousness, "this sense of always looking at one's self through the eyes of others, of measuring one's soul by the tape of a world that looks on in amused contempt and pity" (p. 45). In our work here we are committed to envisioning and enacting pedagogies that are not filtered through a lens of contempt and pity (e.g., the "achievement gap") but, rather, are centered on contending in complex ways with the rich and innovative linguistic, literate, and cultural practices of Indigenous American, African American, Latina/o, Asian American, Pacific Islander, and other youth and communities of color. What if, indeed, the goal of teaching and learning with youth of color was not ultimately to see how closely students could perform White middle-class norms but to explore, honor, extend, and, at times, problematize their heritage and community practices?"

DLI schools carry a historical legacy of honoring heritage languages and community practices. DLI programs went against the grain, resisting English-only ideologies and Euro-centric curricula. Several veteran teachers I spoke to recounted stories of teaching according to their own pedagogical frameworks, linking the lived realities of their students and the wisdom of their communities to everyday schooling. The students learned about their own culture, and cultures around the globe. The teachers also pointed out the many ways art, theater, play-based learning, and music were as integral to the teaching and learning of language as math and language arts. In the words of one educator, "We were left alone to connect with our kids in a lot of different ways. The district didn't care about what we did, we were really left alone which was great in one way because we were able to do whatever we thought was best for the kids, but they also left us alone when it came to support and resources ... if I had to choose though, I would go back to the times when they left us alone because the support came through with moms, small businesses, extended family."

Interestingly, Paris (2014) offers an additional compelling argument that monolingualism and monoculturalism, which is presented as the ladder towards success, may impede access to power. He writes,

> To offer youth full access to power, then, we must understand that power is now based in part on one's ability to communicate effectively to more than "standard" English monolinguals/monoculturals, who are becoming a shrinking share of the U.S. population. As youth of color learn DAE (and other dominant skills and knowledges) and maintain their multiple ways of speaking and being, it is DAE monolinguals/monoculturals who may increasingly find themselves at a disadvantage. CSP, then, is necessary to honor and value the rich and varied practices of communities of color and is a necessary pedagogy for supporting access to power in a changing nation.

Bi/multilingual children benefit from inner wisdom when they let go of the false notion that they are less qualified than others to determine their fate. When children fail to use their innate wisdom, they begin to doubt their truths, failing to discover how intensely beautiful and useful self-trust can be in the classroom. DLI schools can access the wisdom of self-knowledge and deem language as part and parcel of that knowledge.

Inner wisdom allows children to do what they need to do and be who they want to be as multilingual beings. Schools can pave the way for multilingual children to utilize their strengths, acknowledge their innate wisdom, subsequently fulfilling their truest potential. DLI schools share a history of promoting, validating, and utilizing the wisdom that bilingual children bring with them, a history that should not be forgotten.

We Safeguard the Education of Linguistic Minoritized Youth

The intention to protect linguistic minorities may sound less conceptual than the others. Nevertheless, it is an example of an intention that addresses a particular struggle or concern unique to the community. For instance, research shows that White English-speaking parents who want their children to learn another language strongly seek these programs. This complicates race and class dynamics within the school, resulting in DLI programs that disproportionately benefit the English-speakers in comparison to the students who are "ELs."

These DLI schools are situated in a state and country that embark on deliberate policies and actions to reinforce the dominant language and thwart any real attempt to reach a balance between the dominant language and any other language. At the three schools I visited, teachers, staff, and parents understood the dominance of the English language hand in hand with the cultural capital of White parents. As a result, the school community measured their school's success at achieving bilingualism by evaluating to what extent it leveled the playing field between the dominant and non-dominant languages.

DLI teachers were most vocal in safeguarding a just and meaningful education for language minoritized youth. One teacher expands:

> We are constantly making sure our ELs are succeeding at the same levels as our EOs. During our planning meetings, we go over our internal data, test scores, and make sure that we are not recreating the same inequity you would find at a monolingual school. Our ELs, especially if there are SES differences, are the ones we focus on in the sense that we know that we cannot be a successful program if there are gaps in achievement.

Another teacher confirms, "We have to be over the top with Spanish. No excuses. In a 90–10 program, you can't be wishy washy with the language in the classroom. Spanish only 90 percent of the time, and we do this because we know how easy it is for English to become the central language again."

One novice teacher conducted a quantitative study at the school site for his thesis. He was pursuing a Master Degree in Urban Education and was interested in the Mathematics achievement between "EO" and "EL" students. After reviewing the raw data of Spanish speakers and native English speakers achievement on the for the mathematics portion of the standardized state assessment for two consecutive years, he found that native Spanish speakers' performance was considerably lower than their native-English speaking peers despite the fact that they had a linguistic advantage in the 90–10 program in that most instruction in the early years was conducted in Spanish.

When he shared the data with his colleagues, he was hesitant:

> I didn't really know how the teachers or the principal would react. My school is considered a model school in the bilingual community. People take fieldtrips here to observe classrooms. But the teachers were so great about it, appreciative really. No one was defensive. It made the principal realize that they were focusing on reading and writing and making sure the ELs were on par with the EOs. Math was not on anyone's radar, but it showed that maybe we were doing things unconsciously.

My observations confirm that the DLI schools protect the Spanish language. I observed a few kindergarten and first-grade classes during my initial visit to a 90–10 school. The dominant language of interaction and instruction was Spanish. The first lesson of the day began with the students joining the teacher in singing several songs in Spanish. The teacher took attendance and performed other traditional tasks in Spanish. When some of the students could not understand her, she repeated herself in Spanish and used hand gestures and physical modeling to explain—she did not rely on English.

In fact, during an interview with a non-Spanish speaking parent, she recounted an amusing story:

> My kid runs to me while I'm working a booth, practically yelling that Senora A can speak English. Apparently, he overheard her at the school carnival. He was so shocked. He actually believed she could only speak Spanish.

Bilingualism was deeply ingrained in the school culture at each of the school sites. Teachers, staff, and children spoke Spanish and English, in and out of the classrooms, at recess and in the school corridors and offices. One heard Spanish much more than English. Accented English and accented Spanish were evident, but so was the feeling that most were comfortable and confident in speaking either language whatever the level of fluency. The classroom settings—the signs and posters on the walls, the books, resources, and equipment for the children—reflected the language of instruction: Spanish. At one school, however, I detected a significant shortage of Spanish literature, novels and/or poetry written by Spanish-speaking authors. Most of the available literature were simply English books translated in Spanish.

During a focus group interview with four Spanish-speaking parents, they confirmed that Spanish was highly valued at the school. One parent who volunteers daily stated,

Everything they send home is in Spanish. I never have to worry about not getting information or having to ask for something to be translated. Like last week, I went to an awards ceremony for my daughter, and so all the parents were there, some bilingual but some not. It didn't matter because the awards were presented in Spanish and English, and they actually start with Spanish first.

Another parent affirmed, "You know early on that Spanish is number one. That is the language that needs to be protected the most because if you don't, it will be lost. I think that some parents when deciding if they are going to send their child here get a feeling that Spanish is number one and decide it's not the school for them."

One teacher summarized the intention of safeguarding Spanish-speaking youth:

> As individuals, we have experienced language loss, or we have seen other people experience language loss. When you combine that with other issues like being poor, growing up in neighborhoods underserved by schools, it now affects your life in a bigger, I guess more overwhelming way. Now I really have nothing to hold on to, to help me move forward in life. So, if we are about providing an equal education to our students, then we have to recognize that not everyone is coming to our school with equal resources. So, if it seems that we are more proactive about our ELs, then yes we are.

We Honor the Dignity of Bilingual Children

Human rights documents echo the relationship between dignity and the humanity of children. Article 1 of the Universal Declaration of Human Rights declared that all human beings are born free and equal in dignity and rights. The intention, 'preserve the dignity of the child,' emerged from the work of a veteran first grade bilingual educator.

Senora Flores

I cannot state the brilliance of Senora Flores strongly enough. Her ability to deeply understand children and differentiate instruction to meet their unique needs is extraordinary. Her first-grade classroom is a peaceful space where students feel secure, understood, and supported to engage in two languages as young learners. In fact, parents often describe her classroom as 'zen.' There is a vulnerability that comes with language learning, especially in a 90–10 program. Young children will not understand everything and teachers must be uncompromising in their use of Spanish, even if the child becomes frustrated and upset. To ease and support the discomfort of learning a new language, Sra. Flores embraces the whole child.

One parent revealed,

> Sra. Flores will know your child, and I mean really know your child. She's one of those teachers who you sit down with, and as she explains your child's progress, struggles, potential, you immediately feel at peace because she understands every little part about your child.

Another parent, a professor at a nearby university added,

Respect comes to mind. Her level of respect for each child, each family, is so beautiful. You'll never hear her speak about a child or a parent in a condescending or judgmental way. Her mind and heart are open. But I do want to say that it's more than just her embracing your child, she also knows how to teach to your child's strengths. That's the magic of it all, getting to know your child in a very deep way, and then providing the kind of teaching that makes sure the child reaches their full potential.

As a mother-scholar, I also experienced Sra. Flores's 'magic.' Sra. Flores was my son's first grade teacher. Carlo is a free spirit, a curious soul who ponders the big questions in life, who draws bugs and mythical creatures—and who also dies a slow death inside a classroom of rote drill and memorization. Through his K-5 education at a DLI school, I can honestly claim that Sra. Flores was the only teacher who understood and engaged him. She immediately recognized that Carlo understood the material, but needed a quiet space to complete quizzes and the like. She would stay in during recess or after school so he could access this quiet time. She would assess him in non-traditional ways to capture his understanding of the material. Her expertise and 'magic' helped me to understand my son as an 'out of the box' thinker. Carlo is now 12 years old and flourishing in middle school. I want to conclude by saying that Sra. Flores never viewed Carlo as a problem. Not once. And for that—for not dimming my child's light—I will be forever grateful.

In Her Own Words

My uncle, Valentín, often teased me as I was growing up by relating this story at family fiestas: When your tía Cata and I came to El Paso to take you and the rest of the family back to our home in Wilmington, you talked so much the WHOLE TRIP that I thought about leaving you along the way every time we stopped to throw away the baby's dirty diapers. ¡Cómo hablábas!

That facility for speaking in my first language and inquiring about the world around me served me well when I was three years old (even if it sorely tried my beloved uncle's patience). It seems to me now as an adult that I have been on a journey of discovery ever since. H. Thompson writes: "There is nothing more personal than one's language, or his culture. Any attempt from the outside to destroy either his language or his culture strikes deep at the inner core of personality." My parents played a crucial role in determining the formative languages in my life: Spanish and English. My father, born in Jalisco, México, remained until he died, my model for literate Spanish. He was a musician and a voracious reader. My mother provided my first entry into a bilingual world. She was a native Californian with a rich Mexican heritage. She was schooled in the

United States and Mexico—crossing physical, educational and over language borders many times in her life.

Spanish was my first language until the time I entered Kindergarten two months before turning five. In my Wilmington, California neighborhood, I began to learn basic English to play with other children. Fluent and gregarious in Spanish, I had tremendous motivation to transfer those social skills into another language. School, however, precipitated a different type of adjustment. The stages of language acquisition have been fully documented, and studies have shown these to be the same for the bilingual child and the monolingual child. The bilingual child, however, must make additional distinctions to separate his/her two languages. In those cases where the bilingual is not balanced, one language becomes dominant. I grew up in an era when the language of instruction in schools was only English and students were expected to adapt to it. There were quite simply no other options. To assimilate these overwhelming changes, it would seem that the very processes of thought had to change. Where presumably my "thoughts" had been in Spanish, they were now in English. What happens within the heart and soul is even more complicated. The bond between language and identity proves the idea that the first language learned is the one most intimately retained. Growing up, I experienced this phenomenon at critical times in my life. In periods of high emotion or distress, I always reverted to Spanish. The words came so unexpectedly, I surprised myself, but eventually, this process became an epiphany for me. I was aware that an integral part of me was not balanced and I decided to reclaim it.

Education has been a lodestone in my life, and when my youngest son graduated from high school, I took the opportunity to return to college and complete my degree. Working for many years at the Catholic elementary school that I had attended, and now also my two sons, I realized one day that I wanted a career in teaching. The simple act of helping a student who was having difficulty reading and seeing the difference it made as that child experienced success was a turning point in my life. I was hooked! And from deep within me came the certainty that I wanted to teach in Spanish. When I walked through the doors of California State University-Long Beach, after an absence of twenty years, I had the support of my husband and two sons, but I was faced with the daunting prospect of re-establishing my first language. At the time I wrote, "Can the adult acquire language as quickly as the child? Or must it be "learned" in a different context? I am glad to say that I know the answer now. The critical time for acquiring languages, the language acquisition faculty, is in fact that well-documented span of early childhood and the process for an adult re-acquiring language is different. But it is possible, and I know now that embarking on that journey of re-discovery was one of the best decisions that I have made in my life. In my formative years, my home life continuously revolved around a strong sense of family and Mexican cultural traditions as two phonological sound systems played out simultaneously around me. I had a rich context from which to base later decisions that would influence the trajectory of my professional life. I have seen my own life experiences, and a pathway that involved two languages, mirrored in the lives of some of my students and so, I am honored to be a part of the effort advocating biliteracy for all students. You do not have to give up elements of your identity, nor should you have to to be successful. Quite the contrary is true: quality dual language programs—in which language minority and language majority students sit side by side in the same classroom and each acquires the other's language—enrich students' cognitive abilities and their academic performances.

When I was in the teaching credential program at CSULB, a professor interviewed me, asking about my beliefs in regards to teaching. I told her that I believed in respecting the dignity of children. She seemed surprised and asked me where I gained that understanding. I was more surprised because I thought it to be a given. I believe that to this day, and I have added additional insights. I believe that students have a right to maintain their home language as they grow academically and to have the opportunity to develop positive attitudes about themselves and their futures.

I admire my first-grade students for the significant risk they take every day to learn about the world and each other in two languages. An ideal day for me is when I hear the "buzz" of learning going on. Their thoughts and ideas become the impetus for cultivating a shared educational language, and the need for expressing themselves becomes so great that they unconsciously begin to gain expertise in communicating in Spanish and English.

A less than ideal day for me is when I have not had the time to hear a child express a thought or to tell me some personal detail of their lives. Sometimes, my need to "move on" through the curriculum, or even, just to get them to lunch on time, erodes that moment. But, I remember—and take the next chance that I get—to attend to their vast and small moments, and to be a witness to their learning. It is so incredibly exciting and also humbling to be a part of that process. It is truly a stellar moment and quite unlike any other.

As a further testament to the power of bilingualism and biliteracy, I have seen my students grow socially as they learn to respect the cultural and language differences represented in our classroom. By accentuating the diversity, clarifying it and expressing it—my students become more educated every day. We develop a mission statement about what being a Two-Way Immersion student means, and that speaks to being able to meet the affective needs that are so crucial in learning.

Working in the classroom as a TWBI teacher, my mind is constantly tuned to the language groups represented by my 30 students, and I make daily decisions based on their abilities and their needs. I am constantly "unpacking" their linguistic repertoire with the goal of adding new skills to their "suitcase." I am thinking about the student in my class who is a native Spanish speaker and needs to be challenged and advanced to higher levels of Spanish academic work. He may be shy about sharing his expertise, but I know that his traditions and culture are invaluable resources for us.

I may have a student who is new to TWBI and did not have a year with marvelous Kindergarten teachers in the program to ground her. As a native English speaker, she needs to be supported in acquiring the social and linguistic elements of a second language to be prepared for the increasing rigor of academic work. A child who enters first grade with bilingual skills may have an advantage in receptive abilities—understanding in both languages, but not in expressive language. In my opinion, expressive language is a crucial factor in looking ahead to high levels of reading and writing proficiency. All of these students are equally important to me, and my decisions in the classroom revolve around recognizing and bringing to the forefront what they can do and purposefully creating a context for attaining new skills.

The classroom setting provides a structure for the integration of all of these language groups and their varying levels of proficiency. This is an excerpt from the Guiding Principles for Dual Language: While important in other schools, equity is crucial in the two-way immersion program model with its emphasis on integrating students of different ethnic, language, and social class backgrounds. I am not the first educator to state that we are all language learners in the classroom, but I can attest to it.

My experiences, teaching within an additive program model, have demonstrated to me that when language is the conduit, there is a strong cultural component present.

My job is to help students recognize the strengths that each one brings to the classroom community and the fact that we are better together. In addition to the academic nature of our work as TWBI educators, it is evident that the social context is also important. Educators in the field know that teaching to the zone of proximal development guides our instruction (Vygotsky, Lev) as we provide lessons for a child that is just beyond their current level. I have come to understand that guiding and scaffolding the student's social development is just as important because these two systems are interdependent. It makes sense too I look at the affective needs of the child regarding affirming identity and opening the way for growth to occur. Picture that child as an adult. What beliefs about him or herself, language and diversity will a student a "take away" from this classroom? Teaching a student to recognize the extraordinary things—no matter how small—that another student may do in the classroom and give voice to that idea is affirming for both children. Tejus compliments Sebastián for doing a good job as the class mission statement leader of the week. He tells him that the way he guides the students as he uses the pointer is effective because it helps the class read together, and it sounds like a single voice. Sebastián replies that yes! He wants students to read fluently and with expression. On another day, I watch as first-grade students wait respectfully while another student negotiates the meaning in a lesson. Giving a classmate that extra time to speak without interruption helps them understand that everyone has a learning curve and that it may be different for you than for me.

In my first-grade classroom, the topic: What do you want to be when you grow up? Is sure to get students talking in animated voices. First-grade students are experts in sharing their ideas. However, the second question: Will you be able to speak in more than one language in your job? Tell me more ... Causes the voices to pause as five and six-year-old students actually consider how their lives will be different because they are bilingual.

Students of all ages who write about their experiences navigating their world often describe biliteracy as a key that opens many doors. One first grade student writes that the whole world will open up and will be available to him: The gift of self-awareness. An older student wholeheartedly celebrates being able to understand and talk to her grandparents: The gift of legacy and culture. A different student feels a strong connection to the needs of his community and recognizes the obligation to be an advocate: The gift of purpose. Another student speaks to the idea that languages combined with education will change her life and her perspective on the opportunities that may come her way: The gift of self-determination. A different student posits that biliteracy and bilingualism can be a means to equalize race relations and making the world a better place: The gift of ideals.

The voices of my students reverberate and impress upon me the importance of the work that we do together. Recently I attended an event celebrating the graduation of a lovely young girl from the University of Santa Barbara with a degree in Global Studies. She had also studied in Spain and now had important career choices to make. Amid the joyful congratulations and hugs, my former first-grade student said to me: You taught me how to read. That simple statement carries a lot of weight and volume. When do the three goals of the Two-Way Immersion Program coalesce in students? Both Spanish and English were fully internalized within her and the flexibility to switch from one language proficiency to another was implicit in those words.

Intention

- What is the purpose of a bilingual school?
- Why do we commit to biliteracy?
- How do we define success for our bilingual youth?
- How can DLI education address inequity in our society?
- What is the role of literacy as it relates to a just society?
- What should a typical day look like in a DLI classroom?
- What are the optimal conditions for teaching and learning languages in a DLI classroom?
- What role should the arts play in achieving biliteracy?
- What is the relationship between power and language in our community?
- What is effective and meaningful DLI leadership?

CHAPTER 5

Sustenance

A school community requires sustenance to materialize its intentions. If intention is the dream, then sustenance is the fuel. To dream big without referencing the provisions required to bring those dreams to life sets up an unrealistic and misleading scenario for the school community. For instance, we know that restrictive education policies can set limits to what a DLI school aims to accomplish; different communities have access to different resources; so on and so forth. Undoubtedly, sustenance will vary from program to program, but what is absolutely necessary is that we address intention and sustenance in the same breath.

I wrote this chapter on Sustenance with great difficulty. For one, the bilingual teachers I interviewed were hesitant to "complain." I witnessed teachers staying until 7pm; translating Common Core material into Spanish; eating lunch in their rooms while grading; I can go on and on. In spite of this, the teachers insisted on talking about their passion for the work and that everything they do is for the children. One teacher stated, "I've been teaching in bilingual programs for 21 years, and I can say *sin duda* that it is getting harder and harder. I have never worked as hard as I am now. It is too much, but you have to do it. There is too much at stake."

It was also difficult to theorize and write about what nourishes a DLI program when schools function under harsh conditions. It was a challenge to remain hopeful, to not be angered by how much we are asking of bilingual teachers and students, and by how much we are taking away. Accountability and assessment in the present form usurp creativity and intellectualism in the classroom. This weakens teacher and student autonomy in the decision-making processes of what and how to teach and learn. Moreover, the material conditions of teaching and learning are dismal. I frequented classrooms with 35 children crammed into small classroom bungalows, so small teachers' desks were pushed up against the wall to enlarge the space. Longer days, fewer recesses, sugary foods, pressure for high test scores, newly adopted curriculum every few years, demands to integrate technology—leave bilingual teachers and students exhausted and depleted.

More than ever, it is vital that we document how teachers and students in DLI schools sustain their work under these conditions. The material conditions of teaching and learning are as important as the intention of teaching and learning, and yet, in the educational community, we focus much more

© KONINKLIJKE BRILL NV, LEIDEN, 2019 | DOI:10.1163/9789004389724_005

attention on the latter. In the following paragraphs, I highlight two sustaining dynamics in DLI schools: (1) Intimacy and (2) Humanizing DLI Pedagogy.

Intimacy

I learned firsthand how intimacy fuels a DLI program. My 7-year old son left campus one afternoon to look for me. His teacher, Senora Koerner saw him walking alone down the street, and immediately went running to get him. She walked him back to campus to find me. I was so incredibly grateful. Without hesitation, and still breathing heavily from the run, she replied, "Son mis hijos tambien." They're my children as well.

To sustain and deepen relationships around language requires intimacy. Intimacy is the vulnerability that we invite when we come into close contact with each other. It is our sense of empathy for the well-being of each other, our shared pain when one of us is hurt, our listening to each other's stories as a way to better understand.

Children living in relation to one another, rather than using relationships as means to other ends, is to learn in an intimate space. If education is to be soulful, it must seek new ground that situates relations as crucial to knowing and being in the world. A DLI school built on intimate relationships would not "allow" white middle-class parents to use linguistic minoritized youth as resources, as evidenced by several studies in the previous chapter.

The question of how intimacy develops is an important one since it does not happen overnight. It is an organic process that develops over time. At these schools, sharing personal stories about language identity cultivated intimacy. A significant number of teachers at each DLI school personally experienced language loss and language recovery. They shared these stories with their students and with each other. These exchanges facilitated an openness and vulnerability into painful aspects of their lived experiences.

One teacher shared,

> I remember losing Spanish little by little, as I moved from grade to grade. I was never forced to speak Spanish by my parents, so what could I do. Once I moved out and entered college, the regret of not learning Spanish hit me hard. I felt judged by everyone, that the fact that I did not speak Spanish made me less Puerto Rican. I grew up eating the food, *mofongo, arroz con gandules y tostones*, listening to the music, but slowly lost the ablity to speak Spanish with ease. There was also my reality of being dark-skinned, people would just approach me and start speaking Spanish,

and when I couldn't respond, I felt embarrassed. Full of shame. I was
constantly reminded that I was not bilingual. So I went back to school
and majored in Spanish, and it was at that time that I decided to pursue
teaching as a career. I wanted to teach in Spanish and I wanted to work in
a bilingual school. There's no reason, absolutely no reason why you can't
learn Spanish in school.

By allowing themselves to open up to these profound personal experiences,
richer and more robust relationships formed, which at the end of the day,
sustained their hard work with and for bilingual youth. The commitment to
bilingual education emerged from a deeper place because it was personal.

One particular DLI school stood out in regards to its generational legacy.
Every teacher who works at the school made the decision to send their own
child/children to the program.

One teacher states,

> Some of our younger teachers have kids who go to school here now. Us
> older ones had kids in this program years ago. One of the founding teach-
> ers has a daughter who was in the first cohort 25 years ago. So if you think
> about it, we teach other people's children, our children, and our colleague's
> children, which creates a different kind of school and community. We look
> out for each other and for each other's kids, which isn't to say there aren't
> some problems or misunderstandings, but like any family, at the end of the
> day, we protect each other and advocate for each other any way we can.

Another teacher adds,

> We believe in this program with our hearts more than anything. Because
> for me my kids are the most important people in my world and decid-
> ing on which schools you are going to send them to comes down to an
> emotional decision. If I didn't believe in this program I wouldn't send my
> kids here … it's not just me. Every teacher sent her kids here. Can't think
> of someone who didn't!

During the interview with one veteran bilingual Kindergarten teacher, she
mentioned how alumni from the school are signing up their children to the
DLI program:

> In fact today, one of the parents who was sitting in the visitation today
> has a child who will be five next year, and I had that parent as a second

grader. I tell her, you shouldn't be a mom, you're too young to be a mom, because I'm thinking, oh my God, you were in my second-grade class however many years ago. So now we're teaching the grandchildren!

Intimacy fosters a unique academic family. Friendship, support, family, care, were words commonly articulated during the interviews to describe the culture of DLI schools. The narratives below portray this sense of familia:

I feel like we're always there for each other. Whenever one is down, someone else will take over. In our meetings, if somebody can't do something, somebody else jumps in. Or when we know that someone's husband is ill, we do whatever we can. If somebody is sick and can't come in and leave the substitute teacher a lesson, the rest of us get together, and we figure it out. We never let one of our colleagues suffer or fall apart. Our connection is more than just professional. We help each other grow as teachers and as human beings too.

We've been here for a really long time; we have those really tight connections to the point where we do go to each other's personal events in life. Funerals, baptisms, graduations.

When I have a problem with someone, and it sometimes happens, I can let them know. I can express myself. I think the kids feel it. I think they know. They see us going out to lunch every Thursday as friends—as teachers, but as friends—and so I think they get the feeling that we're all friends too and that we're all a family. I tell them, Señora P es mi amiga, and they'll sometimes be surprised, but I repeat it, Sí, todos somos amigas.

One of the things that I think comes to mind is the sense of family or the feeling of belonging. We are a community of people who have the same goal, the same aspirations to be bilingual, and we're willing to do anything to keep that. We've gone through a lot to preserve our program. I think being very close-knit, not only with the teachers but with the parents. We have so many activities but I think it helps to foster and make that such a tight connection. There is a difference when a parent volunteers to help in the classroom with a reading group than when a parent helps with Folklorico. You laugh a lot more when you're dancing! Everybody's involved in something, everybody wants to help with something, there's always something to do. I think that that's one of our biggest strengths, is that we just have so many people who are willing to step up to the plate to do whatever it is, and just make our program stronger and to continue to keep our program alive. Because there have been so many schools that have tried this program, and it just does not last.

Intimacy with and for the Spanish-Speaking Community

Spanish-speaking families represent a vital community within a DLI school. At two of the school sites, Spanish-speaking mothers made their presence known in a variety of ways—reading and writing with children in small groups, supporting teachers by taking over clerical tasks such as photocopying, preparing materials for a lesson, and assuming leadership roles. Some of the mothers continued to volunteer at the schools long after their children graduated. These Spanish-speaking mothers spoke at length about their relationships with the bilingual teachers, citing descriptors such as mutual trust, respect, and laughter.

Spanish-speaking mothers articulated a personal stake in the integrity of the program. They viewed fluency in the Spanish language as an integral aspect of their children's sense of self. They repeatedly expressed gratitude that they were able to access a bilingual program.

These dynamics facilitated and sustained an intimate connection between the Spanish-speaking families and the school. They perceived their presence as essential and valued at the school. As a result of these intimate bonds with the DLI program, the Spanish-speaking mothers ensured the sustained enrollment of Spanish-speaking students and families. Recruitment strategies such as informal presentations for Spanish-speaking parents, neighborhood flyers, and word of mouth efforts in spaces such as the local Catholic Church, contributed to a just and equitable enrollment of a diverse group of children.

At the third school site, interviews with teachers and parents alluded to the decreasing presence of Spanish-speaking families. One parent delivered a cautionary tale about the complexity of protecting linguistic minoritized youth and their families vis-à-vis an increasing White and middle-class population. At this school, in particular, the leadership team failed to prioritize the recruitment and involvement of Spanish-speaking parents as active participants in the school. English-speaking parents filled leadership slots for Homeroom, School Site Council, and PTA.

An English-speaking parent expands:

> There are more White parents with money at this school than ever before, and even though they support bilingual education, it is sometimes for different reasons having to do with giving their kids an advantage. They may talk the talk, but when it comes down to decisions about what is best for their EO child, then you find out that equality is not as important to them. They've set up a Foundation, they host a fancy Gala that caters to parents who can afford to donate, and everything is online and

in English! These events represent the values of white families, it makes them comfortable. Several Spanish-speaking parents have told me that they are not comfortable with baby-sitting, it is not common for them to go out at night without their children. If we listened to these stories then maybe we could have a Gala or Fiesta that was open to children, or another type of event that makes sure everyone feels welcome.

In sum, intimate relationships played a pivotal role in sustaining these DLI schools. Intimacy among teachers and parents was commonplace (in the following section, I address the teacher-student connection). Intimacy requires a level of vulnerability and trust, which when complicated by race and class differences, may develop differently. Thus, DLI schools must keep a watchful eye on how certain groups position themselves at a school to influence school culture. Inclusivity becomes a vital prerequisite.

A Humanizing Dual Language Immersion Pedagogy

Of all the arts and sciences made by man, none equals a language, for only a language in its living entirety can describe a unique and irreplaceable world. I saw this once, in the forest in southern Mexico, when a butterfly settled beside me. The color of it was a blue unlike any I had ever seen ... There are nine different words in Maya for the color blue in the comprehensive Porrúa Spanish-Maya Dictionary, but just three Spanish translations, leaving six butterflies that can be seen only by the Maya, proving beyond doubt that when a language dies six butterflies disappear from the consciousness of the earth. (Earl Shorris)

Formal education has three main components: curriculum, teaching, and assessment. Typically, the standards movement is focused on curriculum and assessment. At the most fundamental level, however, education is the relationship between the teacher and student. Everything else depends on how productive and fruitful that relationship is.

Bilingual teachers, parents, and youth pointed to educational experiences that nourish a child's humanness. I shed light on these educational experiences through the framework of a humanizing pedagogy, and offer insights as to how a humanizing pedagogy impacts the teaching and learning of bi/multilingual youth.

The first scholar to utilize the term "humanizing pedagogy" was Lilia Bartolome (1994) in her article "Beyond the methods fetish: Toward a humanizing pedagogy." Bartolome illustrates how the focus on technical teaching methods (i.e., the 'methods' fetish) in teacher education undermines efforts to provide students of color with an education that is socially transformative, liberating, and anti-oppressive. Bartolome defines humanizing pedagogies as instructional practices that "respect and use the reality, history, and perspectives of students as an integral part of the educational process" (p. 173). A key, recurring theme in Bartolome's work is that an instructional practice is humanizing when a teacher critically interrogates and discards deficit viewpoints of "subordinated" students. A humanizing learning environment is one in which students are treated with respect and viewed as "active and capable subjects in their own learning" (p. 181).

Humanizing pedagogies for Bartolome (1994) also imply instructional approaches in which teachers can interact with students in meaningful ways. For instance, she cites pedagogical strategies such as cooperative learning, process writing, and whole language activities, as well as listening, learning from the varied and valuable life experiences that students bring to the classroom, and mentoring students. A meaningful teacher-student interaction equalizes teacher-student power relations and humanizes instruction by expanding the horizons through which student demonstrate human qualities, dreams, desires, and capacities that traditional schooling often fails to capture.

In the following section, I focus on the humanizing pedagogy of four bilingual educators.

DLI Teachers

During my visits to each school site, individual teachers stood out in that I would hear the same names come up over and over again, with emphatic statements such as "You have to visit this classroom!" They were right. I was able to witness intellectually vibrant spaces for bilingual youth. The four DLI teachers I engaged with were intelligent, loving, sensitive, empathic, accepting, imaginative, lively, colorful, humorous, thoughtful, generous, candid, and charismatic. It was an incredible honor to watch them in action.

Senora Romero

Senora Romero teaches 5th grade and is considered a "creative genius" at her school site. Her classroom is filled with children's artwork, poetry, and theater props. Every inch of space, from the ceiling to the corners of the room are chockfull of creative student work. As one parent stated, "Everyone visits her classroom at Open House, whether your kids are in her class or not."

For Senora Romero, art is an invaluable medium to achieve biliteracy. She elaborates:

> When you learn a language, there is a safety that you have to feel in the classroom because you have to make mistakes on that journey to become biliterate. I studied art history in college, and I do consider myself an artist as well as a teacher, and one of the things that I loved about my art classes in college is how they were taught. There was no right or wrong way, yes there were suggestions here and there on how to improve a technique, but there wasn't this one answer you had to figure out. It was amazing because you felt so free to experiment because you never really had to worry about how the professor was going to grade you. It was more about the process and not the final product. You were so much more focused on your inspiration and what you wanted to do ... That is why I use art all the time with my kids to teach Spanish. My students can let their guard down, and they can feel free to speak, and the best part, is that they're excited to speak Spanish because they're excited about the art they're working on.

Senora Romero shares a particularly poignant story:

> One of my former students, by the time he arrived in my 5th grade class, was already shut down. He didn't think he was smart and he didn't want to participate. He turned nothing in. He had come to the U.S. at 7 years old and enrolled at our school as a second grader. I used all of my classic strategies to get him to open up to me, I really did spend a lot of time trying to figure him out. Anyways, I do this kind of wild art activity to introduce abstract art to the kids. I play different kinds of music, relaxing, soft, punk, techno, this broad range, and the kids paint the way they feel when they listen to the different songs of Spanish language origin. As the activity progressed, I noticed he got up to get a piece of paper and a brush. By the 5th or 6th song, he was painting, he was starting to get into it. There wasn't like a major breakthrough or anything. I still don't know why that art activity connected with him. But art works like that. You just never know how it might set a student free.

There is a natural connection between art and language. At all three schools, the arts were an integral aspect of the curriculum. Theater, singing and dance performances, art and cultural activities were predominant and numerous throughout the school year. Oral language fluency is an important concern in

DLI programs. Students may be proficient in reading and writing, but speaking with fluency is a struggle. Putting on plays, informal conversations while students create their own art, and singing, create opportunities for oral language in a fun and engaged way.

Interviews with students, and in particular with alumni, illuminated the powerful relationship between the arts and DLI education. When I asked alumni to describe their favorite memories in learning Spanish in school, they described in vivid detail their language learning experience vis-à-vis art.

In their own words:

> I still can remember practicing Ballet Folklorico with my teacher during recess and after school. Any time we could we would practice. I loved it, everyone loved it because it was so fun and relaxed and I guess deep down you felt proud of the beautiful music and outfits, and that everyone was learning it even if it wasn't your culture. I still have the dress from our school performance!

> Yeah, Dia de los Muertos was a big deal at my school. We decorated all the hallways, made altars, it looked really professional when it was done, like wow, we did that? There were so many cool stories we read, and on the night the school community came to see it, we were the guides, so we explained different pieces of it all in Spanish. I still know everything about Dia de los Muertos. Ha! Ha! When I moved into my dorm, I brought the little altar I made in 3rd grade with me.

> We put on the musical of Don Quixote and that was not the easiest Spanish to read. I remember reading the book and then translating the play, like the dialogue. But we sang the songs in English. A real bilingual play so that everyone could watch and enjoy it ... It was a better kind of learning for me like I didn't have to worry about quizzes or tests or writing a book review. It was better and more challenging and I was so proud of our work that weekend in performing it.

DLI schools share a rich history of incorporating the arts as part of the roadmap towards biliteracy, a contrast to the present-day focus on reading and mathematics. Integrating the arts humanizes the teaching and learning of language. Bilingual youth develop and deepen their understanding of their own and others' experiences. In combination with reading, writing, speaking and listening, the arts can open doors for high levels of analysis and also challenge students to explore themselves and their surroundings, and thus find avenues for sophisticated comprehension and communication. The arts convey what it means to be human—they challenge the intellect and provide rich experiences in analysis, exploration, reflection, observation, imagination, experimentation, and communication.

Senor Orihuela

Senor Orihuela's reputation is exemplary, not just at the school, but in the state of California. Most everyone I spoke to, teachers, leaders, policy makers, pointed me in his direction. When I spoke to alumni, the students were clear that Mr. Orihuela was the best teacher.

In reviewing his curricula, Senor Orihuela brilliantly maneuvers high rigor through the use of Spanish-origin literature and content that engages the children. He honors the beauty and rigor of the language. He explains,

> I want the kids to gain a deep-seated appreciation for the Spanish language, that there is intrinsic value to develop it and to cherish it like I did when I was a kid. I don't want kids to feel like they're just doing it just because they're in a bilingual program. So in many ways, I think less of Spanish as an add-on, but as a language that becomes part of who you are.

One alumni shares,

> One story stands out, about a blind girl who was ugly and falls in love. Marinela, I think. He was so good at reading aloud, at acting out the parts. I wasn't a big reader, I just never liked to read a lot, never did. But that's what was cool about his class, because he always brought in different subjects, so like for this story we had to research eye diseases which for some people in the class was gross but for me was great! I remember my mom being impressed with the vocabulary I was learning about eyeballs. He just knew how to get everyone interested in literature, even Science geeks like me.

Senor Orihuela's emphasis on colloquialisms are legendary. His storytelling as well. One student shares:

> He's a very funny teacher, he tells stories in a fun way, you're never bored in his class. Anyway, there's this story he told us about a contest his brother and him would have after school. They would run to a tall tree and the contest was who could climb up and back down the tree the fastest. As Senor Orihuela was climbing the tree, he fell. His brother was worried

and asked him if he was okay—he answered, "Gane." That was a classic moment when the entire class just laughed and laughed.

Senor Orihuela's integration of high-level teaching and learning of Spanish in its diverse forms of expression intellectualizes the educational space. This stands in contrast to most literacy instruction in the U.S. which relies on narrow definitions of reading, the role of the reader and the role of the teacher. Most language arts curriculum privileges a "back-to basics" approach which views meaning making as a consequence of successful decoding. Federal policies like NCLB and Race to the Top show partiality to commercial reading programs over the professional knowledge of teachers.

Unfortunately, DLI programs have followed suit. At one school site, reading assessment is quantified to a large extent by the number of words read correctly in 1 minute, with a goal of 120 words per minute by the end of third grade. I remember my youngest son participating in these one-minute reading marathons in his 2nd-grade classroom. Marco is a performer; he loves to read with emphasis and drama—as a result—the 1-minute test became a power struggle between him and the teacher. The program was titled, Read Naturally, and Marco had no problem telling her that the "name is a lie because it's not reading naturally, it's reading like a robot."

Literacy instruction that is prescriptive and stratified is often times geared for certain populations of children. Patrick Shannon (2007) summarizes the rift in equitable literacy teaching practices:

> Students from advantaged backgrounds are taught the social and cognitive methods of reading literature, sophisticated prose, and non-fiction, while students from disadvantaged backgrounds are presented structured opportunities to read decodable texts written only to help students practice the skills being taught. While some students were being prepared for an active role in democracy through an education that allowed for more freedom of choice and expression, still others were receiving literacy instruction that offered a reified definition of literacy that was nothing more than other than basic skills.

The implications of Senor Orihuela's teaching are poignant. His commitment to high-level biliteracy ensures that language minoritized youth access intelligent, engaging, and meaningful language arts curricula.

One student concludes,

> I feel more confident as a Spanish speaker because I have learned vocabulary that some of my family members don't know, and they're from

Mexico. You never feel stressed out in his class even though I am being challenged. It's Spanish all the time. I've had teachers who will sometimes use English, but not him. He's always smiling, you can tell he loves what he does [laughs] as long as it's in Spanish.[1]

Senor Diaz

Senor Diaz is a formidable presence in his 5th grade classroom. He is high energy all the time, speaks with a loud booming voice, and engages his students one-hundred percent of the time. His pedagogical style is without question grounded in critical pedagogy; in fact, Freire's *Pedagogy of the Oppressed*, one of the first books he read in his MA program, forever altered his philosophy of teaching.

He states,

> Paulo Freire's book Pedagogy of the Oppressed, confirmed many of the ideas I had acquired about learning. For instance, I found the notion that learning is self-generated rather than merely receptive especially important. In my experience as a student, teachers focused on transferring a certain type of knowledge, and getting us to endorse, remember, and reproduce it in class and on tests. In my classroom, I believe my kids have an innate capacity to construct knowledge and language. This is what I'm trying to excavate, you know, the wisdom that's already there.

The bilingual students are provided an open, critical space to explore literacy in all its forms, with particular attention to technology and modern forms of expression. The students in his class create blogs to express their interests and perspectives in both languages, but the way they communicate in Spanish or English is open-ended. In many ways, Mr. Diaz sidesteps the tendency in bilingual programs of top down language teachings that center teacher authority and formal language and denies the value of student ideas and interlanguage constructions. Many traditional language teachers refer to much of these students' language as inferior, as gibberish, or as mindless ungrammatical chatter. For Mr. Diaz, the most important thing is that words are genuine and that they aim to understand and name some element of the world relevant to them. The criteria of grammaticality and pronunciation, on the other hand, ignore the importance of the transforming experience involved in constructing language.

Senor Diaz focuses on the form of language, on the meaning that learners construct, which contributes to the essence of the humanizing power of the language learning experience because we hear everything a bilingual student wants to say.

As one student shared,

> He's the coolest teacher I've ever had. He knows almost everything about me, and he's really interested in what I have to say. I can be myself in his class. I can cuss in my writing, I can use the words we use on the street, I can show him all of me. It's total freedom in his class.

Creativity and human well-being—especially the well-being of language minoritized youth—can be seen as a productive relationship. According to Chandler and Lalonde (2008), a strong sense of identity is vital for well-being. Knowing who you are and where you come from, and having the opportunity to practice and express the things that define you as unique, creates an incentive to imagine and care. Moreover, when we consider building an intimate community that breeds intercultural connection and relationship, the creation of art or group participation in creative expressions can foster connections between individuals, leading to feelings of belonging and engagement. For Senor Diaz, his classroom in a space where youth can meet, talk, and share space while creating their own "stuff."

I skyped into Senor Diaz classroom a few times throughout the year. During one of my 'virtual' observations, the students were watching Lyiscott's reading of her poetic masterpiece:

> A baffled lady observed the shell where my soul dwells and announced that I'm articulate, which means that when it comes to annunciation and diction, I don't even think of it 'cause I'm articulate. So when my professor asks a question, and my answer is tainted with the connotation of urban non-suggestion, there's no misdirected intention. Pay attention 'cause I'm articulate. So when my father asks, what kind 'a ting is 'dis? My articulate answer never goes amiss. I say, father, this is the impending problem at hand, and when I'm on the block, I switch it up just because I can. So when my boy says, what's good with you, son? I say, I jus' fall out with 'dem people, but I done. And sometimes in class, I might pause the intellectual-sounding flow to ask, yo, why these books never be about my peoples? Yes, I have decided to treat all three of my languages as equal because I'm articulate. But who controls articulation? Because the English language is a multifaceted oration, subject to indefinite transformation. Now, you may think that it is ignorant to speak broken English, but I'm here to tell you that even articulate Americans sound foolish to the British. So when my professor comes on the block and says, hello, I stop him and say, no, you're being inarticulate. The proper way is to say,

what's good? Now, you may think that's too hood, that's not cool. But I'm here to tell you that even our language has rules, so when mommy mocks me and says, y'all be mad going to the store. I say, mommy, no. That sentence is not following the law. Never does the word mad go before a present participle. That's simply the principle of this English. If I had the vocal capacity, I would sing this from every mountaintop, every suburbia and every hood 'cause the only God of language is the one recorded in the Genesis of this world saying, it is good. So I may not come always before you with excellency of speech, but do not judge me by my language and assume that I'm too ignorant to teach 'cause I speak three tongues, one for each—home, school and friends. I'm a tri-lingual orator. Sometimes I'm consistent with my language now, then switch it up so I don't ball later. Sometimes I fight back two tongues while I use the other one in the classroom. And when I mistakenly mix them up, I feel crazy like I'm cooking in the bathroom—I know. Let there be no confusion. Let there be no hesitation. This is not a promotion of ignorance. This is a linguistic celebration. That's what I put tri-lingual on my last job application. I can help to diversify your consumer market is all I wanted them to know, and when they call me for the interview, I'll be more than happy to show that I can say, what's good, whatagwan and of course hello because I'm articulate. Thank you.

Senora Valdez

Language in relation to, or in connection to, is the power behind Sra. Valdez's work. Sra. Valdez is a third-grade bilingual teacher who was initially motivated to teach because of her own positive experience as a student in a third grade class. Sra. Valdez is known for her limitless energy, her animalitos in her classroom (a bearded dragon and turtles), and her unwavering smile. She is one the smartest teachers I have ever observed in the classroom.

Dialogic inquiry is the cornerstone of her pedagogy. She encourages students to ask questions, which requires quite a deal of patience! But the safety of a classroom that fosters curiosity also means that students can take risks in their thinking. One parent, a psychologist, stated:

She was the best teacher for my daughter because as an eight-year old I felt she was already starting to shut down in school. Her previous teachers were strict in the sense that there was one right answer and the student's job was to figure out that right answer. My daughter is very creative; she started asking questions since she started to talk. Question after question after question. It was exhausting for me (laughs)! With Sra. Valdez, my daughter woke up. She loved going to school, loved her projects. I guess it was because Sra. Valdez loved her mind.

I observed Sra. Valdez several times in the classroom. Questions such as, How do you know this? Why are you thinking about it in this way? Tell me more. One of the most powerful methods bilingual teachers can utilize is dialogue. In the teaching-learning process, dialogue is a bridge between existing realities and new forms of knowledge or experience in any educational endeavor. Dialogue provides a 'way into' the world of bilingual students for teachers. Indeed, there is no other way of properly 'tapping' the unique world of each learner's knowledge and experience apart from dialogue. Through authentic dialogue, learners and teachers, with different experiences and knowledge, critically reflect on beliefs and information; in such dialogue, both have the opportunity to build knowledge.

For Sra. Valdez, language learning in isolation is detrimental. For her, constructing a curriculum that is based solely on the knowledge of two languages often results in prescriptive and de-intellectualized learning. She consistently positions language in relation to other disciplines—Science, Art, and Creative Writing.

Another parent added:

Oh my gosh what an amazing teacher! Especially with writing in Spanish. My son learned to express himself in writing in ways that amazed me. She's just amazing because it's creative writing that allows the students to write about things they are interested in, she actually encourages it. So if you have a kid who loves science fiction as mine does, then that's the writing style he begins to develop in another language.

One student concurred,

I can write any way I want to, any way that expresses my idea. I love to write poetry and I love to start my sentences with small letters. All the other teachers would make me write with capital letters but that's not what matched my idea. She's my favorite teacher, she always listens to me, and stays with me after school if I need more time.

Re-intellectualizing the classroom space emerged as a salient aspect of these bilingual teacher's pedagogy. This has particular implications for our language minoritized youth who more often than not experience de-intellectualized (and thus dehumanized) education. Research evidences that schooling for language minoritized youth involves memorization, drill, and simplistic language learning. Statistics such as the following confirm this as well—although 3.2% of all high school students enrolled in Advanced Placement (AP) mathematics and science, only 0.8% of English language learners enrolled in AP science and 1.0% in AP math (Hopstock & Stephenson, 2003).

I group these teachers as a critical collective who intermingle biliteracy with a humanizing pedagogy. The classroom space they co-construct with bilingual youth is imaginative, lively, humorous, thoughtful, generous, and honest. What results is a vibrant space for bilingual youth, built on relationships that attend to the cultural, intellectual, and social dimensions of their lives. Bilingual teachers understand teaching and learning as dynamically unfolding, comprised of intricate patterns and relationships that are meaningful, rather than mechanistic.

Understanding students' ways of being and knowing, forging nurturing and connected relationships, studying and understanding students as thinkers through examining their written work or discourse in the classroom, are essential facets of teaching and learning for bilingual youth. The labor of love of this select group of DLI teachers can be described as a humanizing pedagogy for biliteracy.

Conclusion

I inherited a pragmatic sensibility from my Caribbean mother, who constantly reminds me, you cannot have it all. Or better yet, they'll never give it all to you.

As a result of this pragmatic sensibility, I constantly pay attention to context, to limitations, to contingency. Hence, a note on materiality.

Vibrant DLI classrooms require specific material conditions. Fair and just material conditions, such as taking breaks throughout the day, time to eat well, diverse physical activities, small class sizes, rich curriculum in languages other than English. There should be formal and built-in planning times for teachers so they may collaborate, deepen relationships with each other, replenish and think thoughtfully about their students. Students should have time to play, to laugh, to direct their own learning, to engage in the knowledge they are truly interested in.

In policy terms, this might translate into:
- Class sizes capped to 20 students (K-8)
- Waiving out of yearly state testing
- Full-time bilingual assistants in each classroom

- Authentic assessments (such as portfolios that promote discovery) in lieu of report cards and grades
- Home-leisure in lieu of home-work
- Multiple breaks to replenish throughout the day

Sustenance

- How do we sustain an inclusive community?
- Which structures, processes, and policies are needed to ensure democratic decision-making?
- What is needed to create an intellectually vibrant classroom space?
- How can we facilitate locally-generated curricula against the backdrop of standards?
- How do we balance the academic progress of students, as measure by state tests, and our own goals of bilingualism and biculturalism?
- How do we ensure rest and replenishment for teachers and students throughout the day?

Note

1 I want to add that after my interview, Senor Orihuela regretted that we only conducted the interview in English. He is absolutely right.

CHAPTER 6

Imaginings

"Things have a life of their own," the gypsy proclaimed with a harsh
accent. "It's simply a matter of waking up their souls."
GABRIEL GARCIA MARQUEZ, *100 Years of Solitude*, 1967

∴

Imagination stands apart from the dialectical link between intention and
sustenance. Imagination focuses on rupture, on new epistemologies and
ontologies that result in transformation.

The imaginings that arise from bi/plurilingual youth—their process of
experiencing, willing, thinking, acting, and becoming—are non-data for the
educational establishment. As we imagine the possibilities of DLI schools,
I explore the potential of returning the locus of language control to bilingual
youth in an attempt to propel a fluid and non-static understanding of how
language, culture, and identity enmesh with each other. Re-centering DLI education around the epistemology of bilingual youth opens a space for their ways
of knowing to inform what and how we teach. In this way, a DLI education
attunes to their language(s) and reverberates their humanity.

Bilingual Youth Epistemology

There has been a steady stream of educational scholarship that advocates for
the (re)centering of youth epistemology in educational policies and practices. As
schools imagine new ways forward, student voice should be loud and clear, front
and center. Unfortunately, this is not even close to being the case in U.S. schools.

The wisdom and insights of bilingual youth can complicate our
understandings of a "an effective bilingual education." Case in point: In a
previous study that I conducted on middle-class bilingual youth, teachers
spoke about their fervent protection of and the strict adherence to the Spanish
language. The bilingual youth concurred, but understood its impact differently.
As I paid closer attention to their insights and experiences, I discovered that
an unintended consequence of the strict language policy was that the bilingual

© KONINKLIJKE BRILL NV, LEIDEN, 2019 | DOI:10.1163/9789004389724_006

youth performed Spanish in academic spaces. At their school sites, Spanish prevailed inside the classroom walls, but outside of the classroom walls, in more social spaces like recess, English prevailed. Interestingly, using Spanish in social situations with peers was uncommon, despite the fact that their friends were also in these programs and also bilingual. In the words of one bilingual youth:

> Yeah we go to the same school, and we learn in Spanish and write in Spanish, but we don't talk in Spanish. I mean we don't talk like in a relaxed way. In class if we have to do a presentation or something like that I use my Spanish, but like at lunch or after school, it's English. The teachers always talk to us in Spanish even outside the classroom and yeah we can answer them in Spanish, but with friends it's different.

In other words, the use of Spanish in more informal ways, humor, colloquialisms, even Spanish texting idioms (like LOL in English) are absent. Presently, all the bilingual youth use programs like Snapchat and Instagram, gaming platforms like Minecraft, and texting to communicate with their family and peers. Interestingly, none of the students use Spanish to communicate with peers on social media.

Paying attention to bilingual youth insights pushes the conversation on how students experience language learning in DLI schools. As we imagine new paths, we must pay attention to the ground, instead of only responding to the top.

Language, Identity, and Culture in Flux

Insights from youth may point us to new iterations of language, identity, and culture. As a result, viewing language as fixed becomes an impediment in creating DLI education that meaningfully engages young students. There is a rich and rigorous literature base that explores language and identity as social constructs. Works on hybridity, in particular, complicate the discourse around multiculturalism—one of the core tenets of DLI.

Multiculturalism, manifested as a celebration and encouragement of "cultural diversity," suggests that "culture" for any given group is an object with clearly defined boundaries and traits that are long-standing, "authentic," and easily observable. Bhabha explains, however, that this concept of an "authentic" culture, even in the context of a supposed celebration of cultural diversity or in an effort of colonial resistance, can be part of a project that effectively provides the subaltern (the most oppressed groups) with an externally-formed identity, not with agency of their own.

To Bhabha and others, any conceptualization of culture reduced to a set of traditions drawn from the past ignores the complex systems of exchange and interrelation that stretch through history, and that also currently take place under systems of imperialism, cultural dominance, and globalism. This conceptualization of cultures as delineated by fixed boundaries also risks essentialism.

In my conversations with bilingual youth, they evidenced non-essentialist thinking. For instance, bilingual youth rejected the EO-EL binary. None of the 23 students I spoke to identified as either EO or EL. All students self-identified as bilingual and emphasized the flowing in and out of English and Spanish. The labels EO and EL failed to resonate with their experience.

Nonetheless, federal and state policies and schools rely on the traditional labels of EL/EO. Even teacher preparation programs define students whose first language is not English as EL. In fact, most of the time new students are classified by parents' responses to a Parent Language Survey which asks (among other things) whether a language besides English is spoken in the home. However, this language survey does not account for the range of a family's language practices or levels of fluency, as some parents might be Spanish-dominant, while others speak predominantly in English and Spanish on occasion. Families who speak multiple languages at home may also be included in this category. For instance, non-English household does not necessarily mean Spanish is the home language; in a number of the homes of children in Los Angeles, Zapoteco, an indigenous language, is the primary language. These parents learned Spanish as a second language and learn English as a third.

Critical studies in bilingualism support these youth perspectives. The construct of emergent bilingual captures how bilingual students perform language learning in and out of school. When we ignore this bilingualism, these students become categorized under static labels of EL. These labels discount the bilingual nuances and richness of language learning (García & Kleifgen, 2010; García, Kleifgen, & Falchi, 2008). As DLI school imagine new directions, the construct of emergent bilingual provides a more complicated and nuanced understanding of language and identity.

In addition, bilingual youth exhibited a tolerance for ambiguous and fluid identity markers. They consistently pointed out their detachment from language identity, but positively, which was different from the majority of teachers and parents who were much more adamant about the non-negotiability of bilingual identity.

The youth were at ease with fluidity. A particular language learner identity was not a permanent marker of their life goals or an all-encompassing marker.

Pilar, a brilliant artist who feels very connected to Japanese culture, most notably through her anime illustrations, does not use Spanish in her drawings, and does not feel pressure to do so. She was much more excited to discuss Japanese culture and how it related to her identity than her Chilean identity.

Daniel, a 12 year old intellect states,

> I've traveled to countries like Mexico and Spain where I could use my Spanish, and it really made me feel powerful to understand what people were saying. I could go to the market with my mom, and I didn't feel strange or uncomfortable. I mean I wasn't completely comfortable but it was a tolerable comfortableness.

Alongside Daniel's appreciation for his bilingualism, he also identified London as his favorite city.

> I felt at home in London. It was great. I would live there. I want to go to Oxford. I guess I probably wouldn't use too much Spanish, or maybe not at all, but that's okay. I'm okay with that.

Because language and identity are not static, homogenous entities—but rather fluid, ambivalent and complex—bilingual schools become sites where the messiness and formidability of youth ways of knowing show the way to the conditions that make learning possible.

DLI classrooms can and should access and promote students to be linguistically and culturally flexible across multiple language varieties and cultural ways of believing and interacting.

Imaginings with and by Plurilingual Youth

The above section points to how capturing youth ways of knowing often challenges how we misname the connections between language, identity, and culture. Thus, as we imagine new directions in DLI, it is critical that we include youth participation in decision-making processes.

Again, new directions in human rights may inform how we include students in collective decision-making in schools. Children's right to express their views was legitimated internationally by the 1989 United Nations (UN) Convention on the Rights of the Child. Recently, the 35th session of the UN Human Rights Council in Geneva centered around 'Youth and Human Rights,'—the recognition of the importance of youth engagement in the implementation of human rights. New conversations highlighted universal human rights as encompassing youth as rights' bearers. A significant development was the UN's appointment of a Special Envoy on Youth, a position now open to young people. This is a step in acknowledging the unique perspectives, knowledge and visions for the future that young people have.

Youth voice and participation in educational policies and practices is also occurring in select countries. In Denmark, the government has emphasized student voice as a vehicle for creating democratic schools (Flutter, 2007) and in New Zealand, youth voice has been one of the several strategies used to foster active and widespread student participation within schools and the local community (Ministry of Youth Affairs, 2003).

In a DLI school, youth voice and participation can challenge the passive role of students within schools and redefine student-teacher relationships as a joint endeavor in learning languages. In many ways, it may counter conventional conceptions of young people as vulnerable, incompetent and immature, and calls into question the deep school structures that reduce students' status to one of compliant dependence without recognizing the extent to which students today already make many important decisions in their lives as a result of our increasingly complex social world. At school, they are denied the opportunity to develop responsibility, express their social maturity, and shape their learning as social actors in their own right.

The distressing trend in the U.S. to strengthen accountability schemes, increase standards through testing and perpetuate deficit and blaming views of students, their families, and neighborhoods, may be overturned in DLI schools that are connected to the aspirations, lives, and needs of bilingual youth. In the end, student voice implicitly references a sense of belonging. Fullan (2002) contends that at the heart of improving schools lies improving relationships in schools. School cultural change, which he argues must precede organizational change, is where students and teachers can be supported in developing their capacities and in extending their perceptions of learning and teaching, so that they can mutually engage in learning that matters to them.

Imaginings

– How do we promote the well-being of our community?
– How do we evolve?
– How do we ensure adaptability?
– How do we ensure bilingual youth ways of knowing and being inform how we educate?

- How do we engage with traditional forms of assessment?
- How do we teach and learn about the beauty of the languages?
- How do we move between self and clan?
- How do we interrogate unequal power relations within and outside?

CHAPTER 7

Conclusion

Children have a fundamental human right to learn in their mother tongue(s). Access to language learning, particularly the language of culture and connection, is vital to one's humanity. This focus on humanness is what brings me to framing the education of learning languages, in this case, bilingual education, under a human rights framework. Human rights allow those of us committed to bi/multilingual education to anchor the conversation in our students' inalienable rights, as human beings, to live and learn their mother tongue.

No longer considered an intellectual burden or learning deficit, bilingualism is gaining momentum as a must-have feature with built-in, multifaceted value that the public is lining up for in lengthy school waitlists. In a state where Latinx are the largest ethnic group, it makes sense to have educational programs to serve the needs of linguistic minorities that want their children to learn Spanish, or even another language, in addition to learning English.

A human rights-based approach to language situates education in a geopolitical framework that claims that literacy is inseparable from other universal human rights, including social, cultural, civil, and political rights (UNESCO/UNICEF, 2007). When constructed as a right, the definition of literacy expands beyond the classroom walls, beyond hegemonic societal constructs, indeed beyond the boundaries of the nation-state. When constructed as a right, the nature of literacy and what it means to "be literate" does not reflect technocratic elements such as the mere memorization of skills, or acquiring functional literacy as a member in a passive democracy. It is not neutral. Rather, to "be literate" means that children recognize their role and responsibilities as right-bearers and global citizens and learn to "join effectively with adults as full partners in governing schools, shaping their own education and resolving dilemmas that arise when competing rights come into play" (Ericson, 2001, p. 219).

Decisions about which languages will serve as the medium of instruction and the treatment of children's home languages in the education system exemplify the exercise of power, the manufacture of marginalization and minoritization, and the unfulfilled promise of children's rights. Stroud (2002) maintains that "linguistic marginalization of minority language groups and their political and socio-economic marginalization go hand in hand" and that "one is the consequence of the other" (pp. 48–49). Political, social, and technical considerations often collide in policy makers' decisions on language medium, schooling, and curriculum.

© KONINKLIJKE BRILL NV, LEIDEN, 2019 | DOI:10.1163/9789004389724_007

TWI has not reached its full potential and that we have yet to explore the possibilities of more emancipatory practices in these programs and these contexts. The present discourse of DLI is status quo technocratic language at best. Below is a direct quote from the U.S. Department of Education, Office of English Language Acquisition, Dual Language Education Programs: Current State Policies and Practices, Washington, D.C. (2015).

This report presents an analysis of relevant research and extant data related to dual language education policies and practices. Dual language education programs are a type of bilingual education program in which students are taught literacy and academic content in English and a partner language. Dual language programs aim to help students develop high levels of language proficiency and literacy in both program languages, attain high levels of academic achievement, and develop an appreciation and understanding of multiple cultures. Recent research suggests that the approach provides more opportunities for English learners (ELs) to reach higher levels of academic achievement than other types of programs (Valentino & Reardon, 2015; Gómez, 2013; Lindholm-Leary & Block, 2010; Marian, Shook, & Schroeder, 2013). Dual language education promises to give students access to key 21st-century skills—namely bilingualism, biliteracy, and global awareness—and because of the expected benefits for ELs, an increasing number of schools are adopting this model.

This book provided a rationale to promote mother tongue-based bi/multilingual education grounded in international normative frameworks, theory about dual language acquisition, and emerging evidence about the impact of mother tongue based bi/multilingual education initiatives. The book also spoke loudly about the ecological conditions needed to implement successful programs.

The following assert the philosophical underpinnings of a humanizing DLI education:

– A humanizing DLI education is centered around the humanity of our bilingual youth
– A humanizing DLI education is highly contextualized
– A humanizing DLI education is relevant and socially driven
– A humanizing DLI education is ambiguous and versatile, and
– A humanizing DLI education cannot be measured by standardized test scores.

DLI can provide (and in many classrooms already do) a space for our youth to live their humanness. Bilingual education is not simply about learning two languages. Bilingual education is a living and breathing experience—"language is a human faculty that evolved with us, homo sapiens" (Li Wei). Language cannot be isolated or separated out from the human condition. For many of our youth, to be human is to be bilingual.

CHAPTER 8

Epilogue

I will always remember the moment biliteracy emerged more transcendent, more beautiful and powerful, in my mind. My father underwent and barely survived a complicated surgery that resulted in a nightmare recovery. He had a breathing tube jammed down his throat, morphine pummeling through his veins, and a bleak look in his eyes. The thought of 'this is it he didn't make it' played over and over in my mind. Regrets surfaced like a raging bull.

My father's mother tongue is Spanish. He was born in 1931 in Madrid, Spain. I brought my eldest son to visit him. Diego. I don't know what it is, that dynamic between a child and grandparent, a young soul on the cusp of life and an old soul on the verge of death, but needless to say, it is a moving and haunting connection.

Diego is biliterate. He is fluent in both Spanish and English as a result of his education in a DLI program. Sitting beside the hospital bed, Diego was able to speak Spanish to his grandfather, who listened and nodded with tired eyes, who despite the maldito tube jammed into his mouth, tightly taped around his face, found comfort in the words of his mother tongue whispered by Diegito.

At that moment, I was unable to absorb Diego's biliteracy as a mere reflection of cognitive or even cultural prowess. No, this moment mirrored something deeper—the bond between human spirit and language. So, I set out to capture biliteracy differently. The book was born.

© KONINKLIJKE BRILL NV, LEIDEN, 2019 | DOI:10.1163/9789004389724_008

References

Ada, A. F. (1993). *A critical pedagogy approach to fostering the home-school connection.* ERIC. Retrieved from https://files.eric.ed.gov/fulltext/ED358716.pdf

Alanís, I., & Rodríguez, M. (2008). Sustaining a dual language immersion program: Features of success. *Journal of Latinos and Education, 7*(4), 305–319.

Alexander, B. K. (2004). Black skin/White masks: The performative sustainability of whiteness (with apologies to Frantz Fanon). *Qualitative Inquiry, 10*(5), 647–672.

Amrein, A., & Pena, R. A. (2000). Asymmetry in dual-language practice: Assessing imbalance in a program promoting equity. *Educational Policy Analysis Archives, 8*(8).

Ani, M. (1994). *Yurugu: An African-centered critique of European cultural thought and behavior.* Trenton, NJ: Africa World Press.

Anzaldúa, G. (1987). *Boarderlands/La frontera. The new mestiza.* San Francisco, CA: Aunt Lute.

Anzaldúa, G. (2002). How to tame a wild tongue. In. G. Anzaldua (Ed.), *Critical convergences* (2nd ed., pp. 28–39). Boston, MA: Pearson Custom Publishing.

Arnold, C., Bartlett, K., Gowani, S., & Merali, R. (2007). *Is everybody ready. Readiness, transition and continuity: Reflections and moving forward.* Background paper for EFA Global Monitoring Report.

August, D., & Shanahan, T. (Eds.). (2006). *Developing literacy in second-language learners: Report of the national literacy panel for language-minority children and youth.* New York, NY: Routledge.

Bartolomé, L. (1994). Beyond the methods fetish: Toward a humanizing pedagogy. *Harvard Educational Review, 64*(2), 173–195.

Bearse, C., & de Jong, E. J. (2008). Cultural and linguistic investment: Adolescents in a secondary two-way immersion program. *Equity & Excellence in Education, 41*(3), 325–340.

Benson, C. (2009). Designing effective schooling in multilingual contexts: The strengths and limitation of bilingual 'models.' In A. Mohanty, M. Panda, R. Phillipson, & T. Skutnabb-Kangas (Eds.), *Multilingual education for social justice: Globalising the local.* New Delhi: Orient Blackswan.

Capotorti, F. (1979). *Study of the rights of persons belonging to ethnic, religious and linguistic minorities.* New York, NY: United Nations.

Carby, H. V. (1992). Policing the Black woman's body in an urban context. *Critical Inquiry, 18*(4), 738–755.

Cervantes-Soon, C. G. (2014). A critical look at dual language immersion in the new Latin@ diaspora. *Bilingual Research Journal, 37*(1), 64–82.

Christian, D. (1996). Two-way immersion education: Students learning through two languages. *The Modern Language Journal, 80*(1), 66–76.

Cook-Sather, A. (2002). Authorizing students' perspectives: Toward trust, dialogue, and change in education. *Educational Researcher, 31*(4), 3–14.

Cummins, J. (2000). *Language, power and pedagogy.* Clevedon: Multilingual Matters.

Cziko, G. A. (1992). The evaluation of bilingual education: From necessity and probability to possibility. *Educational Researcher, 21,* 10–15.

Darder, A., & Torres, R. D. (2004). *After race: Racism after multiculturalism.* New York, NY: New York University Press.

del Carmen Salazar, M. (2013). A humanizing pedagogy: Reinventing the principles and practice of education as a journey toward liberation. *Review of Research in Education, 37*(1), 121–148.

Du Bois, W. E. B. ([1903]2003). *The souls of Black folk.* Chicago, IL: A.C. McClurg & Co.

Fanon, F. ([1963]1967). *The wretched of the earth* (R. Philcox, Trans.). New York, NY: Grove Press.

Ferguson, A. A. (2001). *Bad boys: Public schools in the making of Black masculinity.* Ann Arbor, MI: University of Michigan Press.

Fielding, M. (2004). Transformative approaches to student voice: Theoretical underpinnings, recalcitrant realities. *British Educational Research Journal, 30*(2), 295–311.

Fielding, M., & Prieto, M. (2002). *The central place of student voice in democratic renewal: A Chilean case study.* Oxford: Symposium Books.

Fitts, S. (2006). Reconstructing the status quo: Linguistic interaction in a dual-language school. *Bilingual Research Journal, 30,* 337–365.

Fitts, S. (2009). Exploring third space in a dual-language setting: Opportunities and challenges. *Journal of Latinos and Education, 8,* 87–104.

Flores, N. (2016). A tale of two visions: Hegemonic whiteness and bilingual education. *Educational Policy, 30*(1), 13–38.

Flutter, J. (2007). Teacher development and pupil voice. *The Curriculum Journal, 18*(3), 343–354.

Fortanet-Gómez, I. (2013). *CLIL in higher education: Towards a multilingual language policy.* Bristol: Multilingual matters.

Freeman, R. (2000). Contextual challenges to dual-language education: A case study of a developing middle school program. *Anthropology & Education Quarterly, 31*(2), 202–229.

Fullan, M. (2002). The role of leadership in the promotion of knowledge management in schools. *Teachers and Teaching, 8*(3), 409–419.

Gándara, P. C., & Contreras, F. (2009). *The Latino education crisis: The consequences of failed social policies.* Cambridge, MA: Harvard University Press.

Gándara, P. C., & Hopkins, M. (2010). *English learners and restrictive language policies.* New York, NY: Columbia University, Teachers College.

Gándara, P. C., & Rumberger, R. (2009). Immigration, language, and education: How does language policy structure opportunity? *Teachers College Record, 111,* 750–782.

Garcia, O. (2009). *Bilingual education in the 21st century: A global perspective*. Oxford: Wiley-Blackwell.

García, O., & Kleifgen, J. A. (2010). *Educating emergent bilinguals: Policies, programs, and practices for English language learners*. New York, NY: Teachers College Press.

García, O., Kleifgen, J. A., & Falchi, L. (2008). *From English language learners to emergent bilinguals. Equity matters* (Research review No. 1). New York, NY: Campaign for Educational Equity, Teachers College, Columbia University.

Genesee, F., Lindholm-Leary, K., Saunders, W. M., & Christian, D. (2006). Conclusions and future directions. *Educating English Learners: A Synthesis of Research Evidence*, 223–234.

Gibson, M. A., Gandara, P. C., & Koyama, J. P. (Eds.). (2004). *School connections: US Mexican youth, peers, and school achievement*. New York, NY: Teachers College Press.

Giroux, H. A. (2011). *On critical pedagogy*. New York, NY: Bloomsbury Publishing.

Gómez, L., Freeman, D., & Freeman, Y. (2005). Dual language education: A promising 50–50 model. *Bilingual Research Journal, 29*(1), 145–164.

Grace, G. (1995). *School leadership: Beyond education management: An essay in policy scholarship*. London: Psychology Press.

Grinberg, J., & Saavedra, E. R. (2000). The constitution of bilingual/ESL education as a disciplinary practice: Genealogical explorations. *Review of Educational Research, 70*(4), 419–441.

Grovogui, S. N. (2006). Mind, body, and gut! Elements of a postcolonial human rights discourse. In B. Gruffydd Jones (Ed.), *Decolonizing international relations* (pp. 179–196). Lanham, MD: Rowan & Little field.

Hargreaves, A. (1994). *Changing teachers, changing times: Teachers' work and culture in the postmodern age*. New York, NY: Teachers College Press.

Holm, W., Silentman, I., & Wallace, L. (2003). Situational Navajo: A school-based, verb-centered way of teaching Navajo. In J. Reyhner, O. Trujillo, R. L. Carrasco, & I. Lockard (Eds.), *Nurturing native language* (pp. 25–52). Flagstaff, AZ: Northern Arizona University.

hooks, b. (1994/2014). *Teaching to transgress*. New York, NY: Routledge.

Hopstock, P. J., & Stephenson, T. G. (2003). *Descriptive study of services to LEP students and LEP students with disabilities* (Special topic report No. 1). Arlington, VA: Development Associates, Inc.

Howard, E. R., Sugarman, J., & Christian, D. (2003). *Trends in two way immersion education: A review of the research*. Baltimore, MD: Center for Research on the Education of Students Placed at Risk.

Howard, E. R., Sugarman, J., Christian, D., Lindholm-Leary, K. J., & Rogers, D. (2007). *Guiding principles for dual language education* (2nd ed.). Washington, DC: Center for Applied Linguistics.

Irvine, J. (Ed.). (2002). *In search of wholeness: African American teachers and their culturally specific classroom practices*. New York, NY: Palgrave.

Kirylo, J. D., Thirumurthy, V., & Patte, M. M. (2010). Issue in education: Can you imagine a world without recess? *Childhood Education, 87*(1), 62–63.

Kosonen, K. (2005). *Education in local languages: Policy and practice in Southeast Asia. First languages first: Community-based literacy programmes for minority language contexts in Asia*. Bangkok: UNESCO Bangkok.

Krashen, S. D. (1996). *Under attack: The case against bilingual education*. Culver City, CA: Language Education Associates.

Krashen, S. D. (1999, May). *Bilingual education: Arguments for and (bogus) arguments against*. Paper presented at the Georgetown University Roundtable on Languages and Linguistics, Washington, DC.

Ladson-Billings, G. (2006). From the achievement gap to the education debt: Understanding achievement in US schools. *Educational Researcher, 35*(7), 3–12.

Lambert, W. E., & Tucker, G. R. (1972). *Bilingual education of children: The St. Lambert experiment*. Rowley, MA: Newbury House Publishers.

Lee, P. (1996). Cognitive development in bilingual children: A case for bilingual instruction in early childhood education. *The Bilingual Research Journal, 20*(3–4), 499–522.

Lindholm-Leary, K. J. (2001). *Dual language education* (Vol. 28). Bristol: Multilingual Matters.

Lindholm-Leary, K. (2012). Success and challenges in dual language education. Theory into Practice. *Special Issue: Rethinking Language Teaching and Learning in Multilingual Classrooms, 51*(4), 256–262.

Lindholm-Leary, K., & Block, N. (2010). Achievement in predominantly low SES/Hispanic dual language schools. *International Journal of Bilingual Education and Bilingualism, 13*(1), 43–60.

Lopez, F. (2010). Identity and motivation among Hispanic English language learners in disparate educational contexts. *Education Policy Analysis Archives, 18*(16), n16.

MacBeath, J., Demetriou, H., Rudduck, J., & Myers, K. (2003). *Consulting pupils-a toolkit for teachers*. Cambridge: Pearson.

Marian, V., Shook, A., & Schroeder, S. R. (2013). Bilingual two-way immersion programs benefit academic achievement. *Bilingual Research Journal, 36*(2), 167–186.

Marshall, C., & Oliva, M. (Eds.). (2006). *Leadership for social justice: Making revolutions in education*. Boston, MA: Allyn & Bacon.

McAllister, G., & Irvine, J. J. (2000). Cross cultural competency and multicultural teacher education. *Review of Educational Research, 70*(1), 3–24.

Menken, K., Kleyn, T., & Chae, N. (2012). Spotlight on "long-term English language learners": Characteristics and prior schooling experiences of an invisible population. *International Multilingual Research Journal, 6*(2), 121–142.

Mitra, D. L. (2004). The significance of students: Can increasing" student voice" in schools lead to gains in youth development? *Teachers College Record, 106*, 651–688.

Moraga, C., & Anzaldúa, G. (Eds.). (1981). *This bridge called my back: Writings by radical women of color.* San Francisco, CA: Aunt Lute Books.

Moya, P. M. (2011). Who we are and from where we speak. *Transmodernity, 1*(2), 5–16.

Mutua, M. W. (2002). Terrorism and human rights: Power, culture and subordination. *Buffalo Human Rights Law Review, 8*, 1–14.

Noguera, P. (2003). *City schools and the American dream: Reclaiming the promise of public education.* New York, NY: Teachers College Press.

Orner, M. (1992). Interrupting the calls for student voice in "liberatory" education: A feminist poststructuralist perspective. In C. Luke & J. Gore (Eds.), *Feminisms and critical pedagogy* (pp. 74–89). New York, NY: Routledge.

Palmer, D. (2010). Race, power, and equity in a multiethnic urban elementary school with a dual-language "strand" program. *Anthropology & Education Quarterly, 41*(1), 94–114.

Paris, D. (2009). "They're in my culture, they speak the same way": African American language in multi-ethnic high schools. *Harvard Educational Review, 79*, 428–447.

Phillips, J. K., & Abbott, M. (2011). *A decade of foreign language standards: Impact, influence, and future directions.* Alexandria, VA: American Council on the Teaching of Foreign Languages.

Pimentel, C., Soto, L. D., Pimentel, O., & Urrieta, L. (2008). The dual language dualism: ¿Quiénes ganan? *Texas Association for Bilingual Education Journal, 10*, 200–223.

Popkewitz, T. (2008). Education sciences, schooling, and abjection: Recognizing difference and the making of inequality? *South African Journal of Education, 28*(3), 301–319.

Potowski, K. (2007). *Language and identity in a dual immersion school.* Tonawanda, NY: Multilingual Matters.

Quintanar-Sarellana, R. (2004). ¡Si se puede! Academic excellence and bilingual competency in a K-8 two-way dual immersion program. *Journal of Latinos and Education, 3*(2), 87–102.

Ricento, T. (2005). Problems with the 'language-as-resource' discourse in the promotion of heritage languages in the USA. *Journal of Sociolinguistics, 9*(3), 348–368.

Rodríguez, M., & Alanís, I. (2011). Negotiating linguistic and cultural identity: One borderlander's leadership initiative. *International Journal of Leadership in Education, 14*(1), 103–117.

Rossell, C. H., & Baker, K. (1996). The educational effectiveness of bilingual education. *Research in the Teaching of English, 30*(1), 7–74.

Rudduck, J., Chaplain, R., & Wallace, G. (Eds.). (1996). *School improvement: What can pupils tell us?.* London: Routledge.

Rudduck, J., & Fielding, M. (2006). Student voice and the perils of popularity. *Educational Review, 58*(2), 219–231.

Rudduck, J., & McIntyre, D. (2007). *Improving learning through consulting pupils.* London: Routledge.

Scanlan, M., & Palmer, D. (2009). Race, power, and (in) equity within two-way immersion settings. *The Urban Review, 41*(5), 391.

Shannon, P. (2007). *Reading against democracy: The broken promises of reading instruction.* Portsmouth, NH: Heinemann Educational Books.

Skutnabb-Kangas, T. (2000). *Linguistic genocide in education—or worldwide diversity and human rights?* Mahwah, NJ: Lawrence Erlbaum.

Smyth, J. (2006). Educational leadership that fosters 'student voice.' *International Journal of Leadership in Education, 9*(4), 279–284.

Stroud, C. (2002). *Towards a policy for bilingual education in developing countries* (p. 10). Stockholm: Sida.

Tollefson, J. W. (1991). *Planning language, planning inequality* (p. 234). New York, NY: Longman.

Tollefson, J. W. (2006). Critical theory in language policy. *An Introduction to Language Policy: Theory and Method, 1,* 42–59.

Torres-Guzman, M. E., & Morales, S. (2002). *A profile of dual language programs: A subset of six stable programs.* New York, NY: Office of Bilingual Education, New York City Board of Education.

Trujillo, C. M. (1998). *Living Chicana theory.* Berkeley, CA: Third Women Press.

UNESCO. (2003a). *Education in a multilingual world* (UNESCO education position paper). Paris: UNESCO.

UNESCO. (2003b). *Language vitality and endangerment: By way of introduction* (UNESCO intangible cultural heritage unit's Ad Hoc expert group on endangered languages). Paris: UNESCO.

UNESCO. (2003c). *Guidelines for inclusion: Ensuring access to education for all.* Paris: UNESCO.

UNESCO. (2007a). *Strong foundations: Early childhood care and education.* Paris: UNESCO.

UNESCO. (2007b). *Advocacy kit for promoting multilingual education: Including the excluded.* Bangkok: UNESCO/Bangkok. (5 booklets)

UNESCO. (2007c). *Enhancing learning: From access to success: Report of the first experts' meeting: Defining areas of action.* Paris: UNESCO.

UNESCO. (2007d). *Mother tongue-based literacy programs: Case studies of good practice in Asia.* Bangkok: UNESCO Asia and Pacific Regional Bureau for Education.

UNESCO. (2008a). *Education for all: Global monitoring report. Summary. Education for all by 2015. Will we make it?* Paris: Author.

UNESCO. (2008b). *Mother tongue instruction in early childhood education: A selected bibliography.* Paris: UNESCO.

UNESCO. (2008c). *Mother tongue matters: Local language as a key to effective learning.* Paris: UNESCO.

UNESCO. (2008d). *Inclusive education: The way of the future.* Conclusions and recommendations of the 48th session of the International Conference on Education (ICE), Geneva.

UNESCO. (2008e). *International expert group meeting on indigenous languages.* New York, NY: UNESCO.

UNESCO. (2008f). *International conference on language development, language revitalization and multilingual education in ethnolinguistic communities.* Bangkok: UNESCO/Bangkok.

UNESCO. (2009). *Atlas on the world's languages in danger.* Paris: UNESCO.

UNESCO Bangkok. (2005). *Advocacy brief on mother tongue-based teaching and education for girls.* Bangkok: UNESCO Bangkok.

United Nations. (1948). *Universal declaration on human rights.* New York, NY: United Nations.

United Nations. (1966). *International covenant on civil and political rights covenant.* New York, NY: United Nations.

United Nations. (1985). *Declaration on the human rights of individuals who are not nationals of the country in which they live.* New York, NY: United Nations.

United Nations. (1989). *Convention on the rights of the child.* New York, NY: United Nations.

United Nations. (1990). *International convention on the protection of the rights of all migrant workers and members of their families.* New York, NY: United Nations.

United Nations. (1992). *Declaration on the rights of persons belonging to national or ethnic, religious and linguistic minorities.* New York, NY: United Nations.

United Nations. (1993). *World conference on human rights. Vienna declaration and program of action.* New York, NY: United Nations.

Urrieta, L. (2004). Dis-connections in "American" citizenship and the post/neo-colonial: People of Mexican descent and Whitestream2 pedagogy and curriculum. *Theory & Research in Social Education, 32*(4), 433–458.

Valdes, G. (1997). Dual-language immersion programs: A cautionary note concerning the education of langue-minority students. *Harvard Educational Review, 67*(3), 391–429.

Valdes, G. (2001). Heritage language students: Profiles and possibilities. In J. K. Peyton, D. A. Ranard, & S. McGinnis (Eds.), *Heritage languages in America: Preserving a national resource* (pp. 37–77). Washington, DC: Center for Applied Linguistics.

Valdes, G. (2005). Bilingualism, heritage language learners, and SLA research: Opportunities lost or seized? *Modern Language Journal, 89,* 410–426.

Valenzuela, A. (1999). *Subtractive schooling: US–Mexican youth and the politics of caring.* Albany, NY: SUNY Press.

Wolff, H. E. (2000). *Pre-school child multilingualism and its educational implications in the African context.* Cape Town: PRAESA. (Occasional papers, 4)

Wong-Fillmore, L. (1991). Second language learning in children: A model of language learning in social context. In E. Bialystok (Ed.), *Language processing in bilingual children* (pp. 49–69). Cambridge: Cambridge University Press.

Wright, S. C., Taylor, D. M., & Macarthur, J. (2000). Subtractive bilingualism and the survival of the Inuit language: Heritage-versus second-language education. *Journal of Educational Psychology, 92,* 63–84.

Wright, W. E., & Choi, D. (2006). The impact of language and high-stakes testing policies on elementary school English language learners in Arizona. *Education Policy Analysis Archives, 14,* 13.

Wynter, S. (1979). Maskarade. *West Indian Plays for Schools, 2,* 26–55.

Printed in the United States
by Baker & Taylor Publisher Services